GoodFood
201 One-pot favourites

GoodFood
201 One-pot favourites

BOOKS

10 9 8 7 6 5 4 3 2 1

Published in 2011 by BBC Books, an imprint of Ebury Publishing.
A Random House Group Company
Photographs © BBC Magazines 2011
Recipes © BBC Magazines 2011
Book design © Woodlands Books Ltd 2011

The Random House Group Limited Reg. No. 954009

Addresses for companies within the Random House Group
can be found at www.randomhouse.co.uk

A CIP catalogue record for this book is available from the
British Library.

The Random House Group Limited supports the Forest
Stewardship Council (FSC), the leading international forest
certification organisation. All our titles that are printed on
Greenpeace approved FSC certified paper carry the FSC logo.
Our paper procurement policy can be found at
www.rbooks.co.uk/environment

Project editor: Laura Higginson
Designer: Kathryn Gammon

Colour origination by: Dot Gradations Ltd, UK
Printed and bound in UK by Butler, Tanner and Dennis

To buy books by your favourite authors and register for offers,
visit www.rbooks.co.uk

Contents

Introduction

The *Good Food* team are often asked for new one-pot recipes as it's such an easy and fuss-free way of cooking. With more awareness of where our food comes from, we want to eat home-cooked (and balanced meals), but it's sometimes hard to find time to spend in the kitchen. That's where one-pot recipes are invaluable. A comforting casserole, such as *Chinese-style braised beef* (page 168), or hearty pie, such as *Deep-dish cheese, onion and potato pie* (page 122), make perfect suppers on a cold evening or wintery weekend, and require very little effort to prepare and cook. And one-pots aren't just for the colder months – there are plenty of recipes for warmer days too, such as *Creamy pesto chicken with roasted tomatoes* (page 48) or *Summer pork and potatoes* (page 44).

One-pots are great everyday recipes, and they're also perfect for special occasions, as they're an easy way to cook for friends. All you need to do is prepare your ingredients and put the dish in the oven before everyone arrives, allowing you to spend time with your guests as dinner cooks itself. Slow-cooking will transform cheaper cuts of meat such as braising steak or lamb shanks into delicious bistro-style dishes. If you've got a lot of people coming over many of the one-pot recipes included here are easily doubled, and there is a whole chapter in this new, bumper book of one-pot ideas for feeding a crowd.

One-pots aren't just about slow-cooking, though. On a busy weeknight try *Pepper-crusted salmon with garlicky chickpeas* (page 26) or *10-minute pad Thai* (page 32) – you can make either of them in less than 30 minutes. These quick dishes are ideal after-work recipes, or for when you need a fast suggestion for a surprise guest.

And once you've eaten and enjoyed your main, why not try a one-pot pudding? We've included our favourite ideas here, such as *Rhubarb, ginger and apple scrunch pie* (page 184) and *Cookie dough crumble* (page 186), to satisfy anyone with a sweet tooth!

Notes and conversion tables

NOTES ON THE RECIPES
• Eggs are large in the UK and Australia and extra large in America unless stated otherwise.
• Wash fresh produce before preparation.
• Recipes contain nutritional analyses for 'sugar', which means the total sugar content including all natural sugars in the ingredients, unless otherwise stated.

OVEN TEMPERATURES

Gas	°C	°C Fan	°F	Oven temp.
¼	110	90	225	Very cool
½	120	100	250	Very cool
1	140	120	275	Cool or slow
2	150	130	300	Cool or slow
3	160	140	325	Warm
4	180	160	350	Moderate
5	190	170	375	Moderately hot
6	200	180	400	Fairly hot
7	220	200	425	Hot
8	230	210	450	Very hot
9	240	220	475	Very hot

APPROXIMATE LIQUID CONVERSIONS

metric	imperial	AUS	US
50ml	2fl oz	¼ cup	¼ cup
125ml	4fl oz	½ cup	½ cup
175ml	6fl oz	¾ cup	¾ cup
225ml	8fl oz	1 cup	1 cup
300ml	10fl oz/½ pint	½ pint	1¼ cups
450ml	16fl oz	2 cups	2 cups/1 pint
600ml	20fl oz/1 pint	1 pint	2½ cups
1 litre	35fl oz/1¾ pints	1¾ pints	1 quart

APPROXIMATE WEIGHT CONVERSIONS
• All the recipes in this book list both imperial and metric measurements. Conversions are approximate and have been rounded up or down. Follow one set of measurements only; do not mix the two.
• Cup measurements, which are used by cooks in Australia and America, have not been listed here as they vary from ingredient to ingredient. Kitchen scales should be used to measure dry/solid ingredients.

Good Food are concerned about sustainable sourcing and animal welfare so where possible we use organic ingredients, humanely reared meats, sustainably caught fish, free-range chickens and eggs and unrefined sugar.

SPOON MEASURES
Spoon measurements are level unless otherwise specified.
• 1 teaspoon (tsp) = 5ml
• 1 tablespoon (tbsp) = 15ml
• 1 Australian tablespoon = 20ml (cooks in Australia should measure 3 teaspoons where 1 tablespoon is specified in a recipe)

Autumn vegetable soup, page 16

Simple suppers

Chilled pea and watercress soup

No chopping must make this the easiest soup in the book! Try blitzing the soup with handful of mint leaves for an extra-fresh flavour.

TAKES 10–15 MINUTES • SERVES 4

454g pack frozen peas
85g bag trimmed watercress, roughly torn
850ml/1½ pints vegetable stock
grated zest and juice of 1 small lemon
4 tbsp natural yogurt
ice cubes, to serve

1 Put all the ingredients, except the yogurt and ice, in a blender. Don't overfill your machine – you may need to do this in two batches. Whizz everything for a couple of minutes until smooth and speckled with the watercress.
2 Season if you want to, then serve straight away or chill until needed. The soup will keep in an airtight container in the fridge for up to 2 days (give it a stir before serving) or can be frozen for up to 1 month.
3 Serve drizzled with yogurt and drop in an ice cube or two to make it even more refreshing.

PER SERVING 86 kcals, protein 8g, carbs 11g, fat 1g, sat fat 1g, fibre 6g, added sugar none, salt 0.73g

Summery soup with pesto

Pesto and Parmesan add flavour to this simple and healthy soup. Stir in the zest of a lemon at the end for even more of a zing.

TAKES 15–20 MINUTES • SERVES 4

1 courgette, halved and very thinly sliced
200g/7oz frozen peas
250g bag ready-cooked basmati rice
100g bag baby leaf spinach
600ml/1 pint vegetable or chicken stock
4 tbsp pesto, to garnish
olive oil, for drizzling (optional)
grated Parmesan, for sprinkling
crusty bread, to serve

1 Tip the courgette and peas into a large bowl and cover with boiling water. Cover the bowl, then leave for 3 minutes until the vegetables have softened slightly.
2 Drain the vegetables, then put back into the bowl along with the rice and spinach leaves. Pour over the hot stock, then cover and leave for another 2 minutes until the rice is heated through and the spinach has wilted.
3 Season to taste, then ladle the soup into serving bowls. Add a swirl of pesto, olive oil, if using, and the grated Parmesan. Serve with crusty bread.

PER SERVING 176 kcals, protein 9g, carbs 25g, fat 5g, sat fat 2g, fibre 4g, added sugar none, salt 1.4g

Chilled pea and watercress soup

Summery soup with pesto

Moroccan chickpea soup

An unusual and tasty dish for vegetarians. For meat-lovers, fry 4 sliced chorizo sausages along with the onions and celery.

TAKES 20–25 MINUTES • SERVES 4

1 tbsp olive oil
1 medium onion, chopped
2 celery sticks, chopped
2 tsp ground cumin
600ml/1 pint vegetable stock
400g can chopped tomatoes with garlic
400g can chickpeas, drained and rinsed
100g/3½oz frozen broad beans
grated zest and juice ½ lemon
large handful of coriander or parsley
flatbread, to serve

1 Heat the oil in a large saucepan, then fry the onion and celery gently for 10 minutes until softened, stirring frequently. Tip in the cumin and fry for another minute.
2 Turn up the heat, then add the stock, tomatoes and chickpeas, plus a good grind of black pepper. Simmer for 8 minutes. Throw in the broad beans and lemon juice and cook for a further 2 minutes.
3 Season to taste, then top with a sprinkling of lemon zest and chopped herbs. Serve with flatbread.

PER SERVING 148 kcals, protein 9g, carbs 17g, fat 5g, sat fat 1g, fibre 6g, added sugar none, salt 1.07g

Cannellini bean soup

For a prepare-ahead dinner-party starter, freeze the soup at the end of stage 2 and reheat just before serving.

TAKES ABOUT 1 HOUR • SERVES 6

1 tbsp olive oil
4 shallots, finely chopped
2 garlic cloves, finely chopped
1 carrot, finely chopped
2 celery sticks, finely chopped
2 leeks, finely chopped
140g/5oz streaky bacon, finely chopped
1.4 litres/2½ pints chicken or vegetable stock
2 bay leaves
2 tsp chopped fresh oregano or marjoram or
  ½ tsp dried
2 x 425g cans cannellini beans, drained and
  rinsed
TO GARNISH
handful of flat-leaf parsley, chopped
extra virgin olive oil
6 parsley sprigs

1 Heat the oil in a large saucepan and tip in the shallots, garlic, carrot, celery, leeks and bacon. Cook over a medium heat for 5–7 minutes, stirring occasionally, until softened but not browned.
2 Pour in the stock, then add the bay leaves and oregano or marjoram. Season and bring to the boil, cover the pan and simmer gently for 15 minutes. Tip in the beans, cover again and simmer for a further 5 minutes.
3 To serve, taste for seasoning and swirl in the chopped parsley. Ladle into warm bowls and top each with a drizzle of olive oil and a parsley sprig.

PER SERVING 214 kcals, protein 13g, carbs 19g, fat 10g, sat fat 3g, fibre 6g, added sugar none, salt 1.78g

Cannellini bean soup

Moroccan chickpea soup

Three green vegetable soup

The just wilted watercress and mint add a fresh and peppery flavour to this speedy, tasty soup.

TAKES 15 MINUTES • SERVES 4

knob of butter or splash of olive oil
bunch of spring onions, chopped
3 courgettes, chopped
200g/7oz podded fresh or frozen peas
850ml/1½ pints vegetable stock
85g bag trimmed watercress
large handful of fresh mint
2 rounded tbsp Greek yogurt, plus extra
    to serve

1 Heat the butter or oil in a large saucepan, add the spring onions and courgettes and stir well. Cover and cook for 3 minutes, add the peas and stock and return to the boil. Cover and simmer for a further 4 minutes, then remove from the heat and stir in the watercress and mint until they are wilted.
2 Purée in the pan with a hand blender, adding the yogurt halfway through. Add seasoning to taste. Serve hot or cold, drizzled with extra yogurt.

PER SERVING 100 kcals, protein 8g, carbs 9g, fat 4g, sat fat 2g, fibre 4g, added sugar none, salt 0.81g

White bean soup with chilli oil

The perfect soup to start a Sunday lunch in winter. The chilli oil is the perfect foil to the mealiness of the beans.

TAKES 1½–1¾ HOURS, PLUS OVERNIGHT SOAKING • SERVES 6

500g/1lb 2oz dried butter beans, soaked
    overnight
2 tbsp vegetable oil
1 medium onion, chopped
1 garlic clove, chopped
2 carrots, chopped
2 celery sticks, chopped
1.4 litres/2½ pints vegetable stock
2 bay leaves
2–3 fresh thyme sprigs, plus extra for sprinkling
chilli oil, for drizzling

1 Drain the beans. Shuck off and discard the skins by pinching the beans between finger and thumb. Put the beans in a colander, rinse and drain.
2 Heat the oil in a pan and fry the onion and garlic for 1–2 minutes. Tip in the carrots and celery and fry gently for 2–3 minutes. Add the beans, stock, bay and thyme with some pepper, and bring to the boil. Reduce the heat, cover and simmer for 20–25 minutes, skimming off any scum, until the beans are soft.
3 Cool the soup for 10 minutes, discard the bay and thyme, then purée in the pan with a hand blender until quite smooth. Check for seasoning and reheat if necessary, then serve with a drizzle of chilli oil and a sprinkling of thyme leaves.

PER SERVING 319 kcals, protein 18g, carbs 49g, fat 7g, sat fat 1g, fibre 15g, added sugar none, salt 0.89g

Three green vegetable soup

White bean soup with chilli oil

Provençal tomato soup

Nothing compares with freshly made tomato soup. Wait until the autumn when tomatoes are at their tastiest.

TAKES 1½–1¾ HOURS • SERVES 4

2 tbsp olive oil
1 onion, finely chopped
1 carrot, finely chopped
1 celery stick, finely chopped
2 tsp tomato purée, plus to taste
1kg/2lb 4oz ripe tomatoes, quartered
2 bay leaves
good pinch of sugar, or to taste
1.2 litres/2 pints vegetable stock
TO SERVE (OPTIONAL)
4 tbsp crème fraîche
small handful of basil leaves

1 Heat the oil in a large saucepan and gently fry the onion, carrot and celery for 10 minutes until softened and lightly coloured. Stir in the tomato purée. Tip in the tomatoes and add the bay leaves and sugar. Season to taste. Stir well, cover and cook gently for 10 minutes until the tomatoes reduce down slightly.

2 Pour in the stock, stir and bring to the boil. Cover and cook gently for 30 minutes, stirring once or twice. Remove the bay leaves. Purée the soup in the pan with a hand blender until fairly smooth, then pour through a sieve to remove the tomato skins and seeds.

3 Return the soup to the pan and reheat. Taste and add more sugar, and salt and pepper if you like, plus some more tomato purée for a deeper colour. Serve hot, topped with crème fraîche and basil leaves, if you like.

PER SERVING 124 kcals, protein 4g, carbs 13g, fat 7g, sat fat 0.9g, fibre 3.7g, added sugar 0.5g, salt 1.09g

Autumn vegetable soup

A great soup for freezing ahead. Just reheat, make cheese on toast, if you like – it's very tasty with Edam – and serve.

TAKES 30–40 MINUTES • SERVES 4

1 leek, chopped quite small
2 carrots, chopped quite small
1 potato, peeled and chopped quite small
1 garlic clove, finely chopped
1 tbsp finely chopped fresh rosemary
425ml/¾ pint vegetable stock
½ tsp sugar
2 x 400g cans chopped tomatoes
410g can chickpeas, drained and rinsed
3 tbsp chopped fresh parsley
cheese on toast or buttered toast, to serve
    (optional)

1 Put the vegetables into a large saucepan with the garlic, rosemary, stock and sugar. Season and stir well, then bring to a simmer. Cover and cook gently for 15 minutes or until the vegetables are just tender.

2 Whizz the tomatoes in a food processor or blender until smooth, then tip into the vegetables with the chickpeas and parsley. Gently heat through, stirring now and then. Taste for seasoning and serve hot – with cheese on toast or buttered toast, if you like.

PER SERVING 151 kcals, protein 9g, carbs 25g, fat 2g, sat fat none, fibre 6.9g, added sugar 0.7g, salt 1.14g

Smoked haddock chowder

To give this simple, healthy soup a kick, add a dash of Tabasco sauce.

TAKES 20–25 MINUTES • SERVES 2

1 onion, chopped
2 potatoes, scrubbed and sliced
500ml/18fl oz vegetable stock
2 smoked haddock fillets, about
100g/3½oz each, cut into chunks
418g can creamed corn
milk, to taste
handful of parsley, chopped (optional)

1 Put the onion and potatoes into a large sauté pan. Pour over the vegetable stock and simmer for 6–8 minutes until the potatoes are soft, but still have a slight bite. Add the chunks of smoked haddock. Tip in the creamed corn and add a little milk if you like a thick chowder, more if you like it thinner.
2 Gently simmer for 5–7 minutes until the haddock is cooked (it should flake when prodded with a fork). Sprinkle over the parsley, if using, and ladle the chowder into bowls.

PER SERVING 555 kcals, protein 37g, carbs 84g, fat 10g, sat fat 3g, fibre 7g, added sugar none, salt 0.3g

Perky turkey soup

A brilliant way of using up Christmas leftovers. And the spicy flavours make a welcome change.

TAKES 25–35 MINUTES • SERVES 4

1 tbsp olive oil
1 large onion, halved and sliced into thin strips
1 red pepper, deseeded and sliced into thin
    strips
2 tsp ground coriander
¼ –½ tsp chilli flakes
3 tbsp basmati or long-grain rice
1.5 litres/2¾ pints turkey or chicken stock
250g/9oz cooked turkey meat, cut into thin
    strips
410g can chickpeas, drained and rinsed
handful of fresh coriander or flat-leaf parsley,
    roughly chopped

1 Heat the oil in a large saucepan, add the onion and fry for 5 minutes or so, stirring every now and then until it starts to soften.
2 Add the red pepper, ground coriander, chilli and rice and stir for about 1 minute. Pour in the hot stock, stir in the turkey and chickpeas and season well. Bring to the boil, cover and simmer for 8–10 minutes, until the vegetables and rice are tender. Stir in the fresh coriander or parsley and serve.

PER SERVING 291 kcals, protein 27g, carbs 27g, fat 9g, sat fat 2g, fibre 4g, added sugar none, salt 1.78g

Chunky winter broth

This hearty winter supper is a great way of getting your daily vitamins.

TAKES 15–20 MINUTES • SERVES 4

2 x 400g cans chopped tomatoes
2 litres/3½ pints vegetable stock
4 carrots, sliced
2 x 400g cans mixed pulses, drained and rinsed
175g/6oz spinach leaves
1 tbsp roasted red pepper pesto
crusty bread, to serve

1 Tip the tomatoes into a large saucepan along with the stock. Bring to the boil, turn down the heat and throw in the carrots. Gently simmer the soup until the carrots are cooked, about 15 minutes.
2 Add the pulses and spinach and heat for a few minutes, stirring, until the spinach has wilted. Spoon in the pesto and gently mix into the soup. Serve with some crusty bread.

PER SERVING 219 kcals, protein 16g, carbs 34g, fat 3g, sat fat 3g, fibre 12g, added sugar none, salt 3.16g

Broccoli soup with goat's cheese

This is a great warming lunch or starter. If you don't like goat's cheese, try Brie instead.

TAKES 40–50 MINUTES • SERVES 4

50g/2oz butter
1 large onion, finely chopped
900g/2lb broccoli, chopped (keep florets and
   stalks separate)
generous grating of fresh nutmeg or ¼ tsp
   ground nutmeg
1 litre/1¾ pints vegetable or chicken stock
600ml/1 pint full-fat milk
100g/3½oz medium-soft goat's cheese,
   chopped (rind and all)
croûtons, to serve (optional)

1 Melt the butter in a large saucepan, add the onion, broccoli stalks and nutmeg and fry for 5 minutes until soft. Add the broccoli florets and stock, then the milk. Cover and simmer gently for 8 minutes until the broccoli is tender.
2 Take out about four ladlefuls of broccoli, then purée the rest in the pan with a hand blender until smooth. Return the reserved broccoli to the soup and check for seasoning. (The soup will keep in the fridge for 2 days or you can cool it and freeze it for up to 2 months.)
3 To serve, reheat if necessary and scatter with the goat's cheese – and croûtons if you like.

PER SERVING 371 kcals, protein 22g, carbs 16g, fat 25g, sat fat 14.5g, fibre 6.6g, added sugar none, salt 1.67g

Chunky winter broth

Broccoli soup with goat's cheese

Mexican soup with chicken

The fun of this fresh spicy soup is that everyone can add whatever they like to their own bowl. Don't hold back, as it's low in fat, too.

TAKES 30 MINUTES • SERVES 4

2 tbsp olive oil
1 onion, chopped
4 garlic cloves, crushed
a pinch of dried chilli flakes
½ tsp ground cumin
400g can plum tomatoes
1.5 litres/2¾ pints chicken stock
2 skinless chicken breasts, sliced (or use
    leftover cooked chicken)
juice 2 limes
FOR THE TOPPINGS
tortilla chips, chopped avocado, lime wedges,
    red onion and coriander leaves

1 Heat the oil in a large pan. Add the onion and garlic, soften for 5 minutes, then stir in the chilli, cumin, tomatoes and chicken stock. Blitz in a food processor in batches, or use a hand blender to purée until smooth.
2 Return to the pan, then bring to the boil. If using raw chicken, add then reduce the heat and simmer for 10 minutes until cooked through. If using cooked, simply warm through. Stir in the lime juice and some seasoning, then ladle into bowls. Put the toppings in the middle of the table for everyone to help themselves.

PER SERVING (soup only) 257kcals, protein 34g, carbs 10g, fat 10g, sat fat 1g, fibre 2g, sugar 6g, salt 2.12g

Sweet potato and rosemary soup

This rustic soup is super quick and cheap to make, but full of flavour. Leave it chunky or whizz it until silky smooth – the choice is yours.

TAKES 30 MINUTES • SERVES 4

2 tsp olive oil, plus extra for brushing
1 onion, chopped
2 garlic cloves, crushed
750g/1lb 10oz sweet potatoes, peeled and
    cubed
1 litre/1¾ pints vegetable or chicken stock, plus
    extra (if needed)
1 fresh rosemary sprig, plus extra to garnish
toasted bread, to serve

1 Heat the oil in a large pan, then fry the onion for 5 minutes until soft. Add the garlic, then fry for 1 minute more. Stir in the sweet potatoes, then cover with the stock and bring to the boil. Strip the leaves from the rosemary sprig, and add them to the pan. Simmer for 10 minutes until the potato is soft.
2 Use a hand blender to purée the soup, adding a splash more hot water or stock if it seems too thick. Season well, then pour into warmed bowls and serve with toasted bread and a few leaves of rosemary, if you like.

PER SERVING 253 kcals, protein 13g, carbs 45g, fat 4g, sat fat 0.4g, fibre 6g, sugar 13g, salt 1.46g

Mexican soup with chicken

Sweet potato and rosemary soup

Thai chicken and coconut soup

For an even more authentic meal, serve this rich and creamy soup with some ready-cooked Thai fragrant rice.

TAKES 35–40 MINUTES • SERVES 4

2 x 400g cans coconut milk
3 tbsp fish sauce
4cm/1½in piece fresh root ginger or galangal, peeled and finely chopped
2 lemongrass stalks, finely sliced
6 kaffir lime leaves or strips of lime zest
1 fresh red chilli, chopped
2 tsp light muscovado sugar
500g/1lb 2oz boneless, skinless chicken breasts, cut into small bite-size pieces
2 tbsp lime juice
good handful of fresh basil and coriander, roughly chopped

1 Tip all the ingredients except the chicken, lime juice and herbs into a large saucepan, bring to a gentle simmer and cook uncovered in a relaxed bubble for 5 minutes.
2 Add the chicken, cover and simmer for 8–10 minutes or until tender. Stir in the lime juice, then scatter over the herbs before serving.

PER SERVING 479 kcals, protein 35g, carbs 10g, fat 34g, sat fat 28.3g, fibre none, added sugar 2.8g, salt 2.96g

Chorizo and chickpea soup

For an Indian version of this spicy soup, use some cooked chicken and a teaspoon of curry paste instead of the chorizo.

TAKES 10 MINUTES • SERVES 2

400g can chopped tomatoes
110g pack chorizo sausage (unsliced)
140g/5oz wedge Savoy cabbage
sprinkling of dried chilli flakes
410g can chickpeas, drained and rinsed
1 chicken or vegetable stock cube
crusty bread or garlic bread, to serve

1 Put a medium pan on the heat and tip in the tomatoes followed by a canful of water. While the tomatoes are heating, quickly chop the chorizo into chunky pieces (removing any skin) and shred the cabbage.
2 Pile the chorizo and cabbage into the pan with the chilli flakes and chickpeas, then crumble in the stock cube. Stir well, cover and leave to bubble over a high heat for 6 minutes or until the cabbage is just tender. Ladle into bowls and eat with crusty or garlic bread.

PER SERVING 366 kcals, protein 23g, carbs 30g, fat 18g, sat fat 5g, fibre 9g, added sugar 0.3g, salt 4.26g

Chorizo and chickpea soup

Thai chicken and coconut soup

Roast chicken soup

Turn your leftover chicken into a hearty soup, finished with a delicious fresh swirl of creamy lemon and garlic Greek yogurt.

TAKES 40 MINUTES • SERVES 4

1 tbsp olive oil
2 onions, chopped
3 medium carrots, chopped
1 tbsp fresh thyme leaves, roughly chopped
1.4 litres/2½ pints chicken stock
300g/10oz leftover roast chicken, shredded
    and skin removed
200g/7oz frozen peas
3 tbsp Greek yogurt
1 garlic clove, crushed
squeeze of fresh lemon juice
crusty bread, to serve

1 Heat the oil in a large heavy-based pan. Add the onions, carrots and thyme, then gently fry for 15 minutes. Stir in the stock, bring to a boil, cover, then simmer for 10 minutes.
2 Add the chicken. Remove half the soup mixture and purée it with a stick blender. Tip back into the pan with the rest of the soup, the peas and some seasoning, then simmer for 5 minutes until hot through.
3 Mix together the yogurt, garlic and lemon juice. Swirl into the soup once spooned into bowls, then serve with crusty bread.

PER SERVING 339 kcals, protein 39g, carbs 18g, fat 13g, sat fat 3g, fibre 6g, sugar 11g, salt 2g

Cheese, bacon and onion puff

Bake a basic batter mixture with a few added ingredients for a simple family supper from the storecupboard.

TAKES 50 MINUTES • SERVES 4

140g/5oz plain flour
4 eggs
200ml/7fl oz milk
butter, for greasing
2 tbsp finely grated Parmesan
8 rashers ready-cooked streaky bacon or
    3 slices ham, chopped
4 spring onions, thinly sliced
140g/5oz Cheddar, grated

1 Preheat the oven to 230C/210C fan/gas 8. To make the batter, tip the flour into a bowl and beat in the eggs until smooth. Gradually add the milk and carry on beating until the mix is completely lump free. Grease a large, round ceramic dish, about 22cm wide, and dust it with the grated Parmesan.
2 Tip the bacon or ham, onions and Cheddar into the batter, and stir until completely combined. Tip the batter into the prepared dish so it comes almost to the top, then bake for 30–35 minutes until puffed up and golden. Bring it to the table and serve piping hot, straight from the dish.

PER SERVING 680 kcals, protein 27g, carbs 30g, fat 51g, sat fat 18g, fibre 1g, sugar 3g, salt 2.15g

Beetroot, spinach and goat's cheese couscous

This colourful and filling salad makes a satisfying supper. Perfect for packed lunches too as it transports really well.

TAKES 10 MINUTES • SERVES 2 (EASILY DOUBLED)

zest and juice of 1 large orange
140g/5oz couscous
25g/1oz walnut pieces
85g/3oz firm goat's cheese, crumbled
6 dried apricots, roughly chopped
4 small cooked beetroot, quartered
2 tbsp extra-virgin olive oil
juice ½ lemon
2 handfuls of spinach leaves

1 Put the orange zest, juice and around 100ml/3½fl oz water in a medium pan and bring to the boil. Turn off the heat, tip in the couscous, mix well, then cover and leave to absorb for 5 minutes.
2 Fluff up the grains with a fork, then add the walnuts, cheese, apricots, beetroot and some seasoning. Mix in the oil and lemon juice (or use your favourite bought vinaigrette). If you're eating straight away, toss in the spinach now; if not, pack into a container with the spinach sat on top. When ready to eat, toss the spinach through.

PER SERVING 601 kcals, protein 21g, carbs 57g, fat 34g, sat fat 11g, fibre 5g, sugar 22g, salt 1.13g

Spicy tomato chicken

All this quick-and-easy chicken dish needs is a big hunk of crusty bread on the side. It's versatile too; try it stirred through pasta or as a topping for a baked potato.

TAKES 30 MINUTES • SERVES 4

2 tbsp seasoned plain flour
1 tsp chilli powder
8 boneless chicken thighs
1 tbsp vegetable oil
1 onion, chopped
600ml/1 pint chicken stock
2 garlic cloves, chopped
2 tbsp tomato purée
2 courgettes, cut into chunks
450g/1lb tomatoes, quartered
small handful of fresh basil leaves, to serve

1 Mix together the seasoned flour and chilli powder. Add the chicken and toss to coat. Set aside the seasoned flour. Heat the oil in a large frying pan with a lid, add the chicken and fry for 8 minutes, until well browned, turning once. Transfer to a plate.
2 Add the onion to the pan and fry for around 5 minutes. Sprinkle over the reserved seasoned flour and cook for 1 minute, stirring all the time. Stir in the stock, garlic and tomato purée. Return the chicken to the pan and bring to the boil. Add the courgettes and tomatoes, cover and simmer for 15 minutes. Scatter with fresh basil leaves and serve.

PER SERVING 424 kcals, protein 33g, carbs 19g, fat 25g, sat fat 7g, fibre 3g, added sugar none, salt 1.2g

Pepper-crusted salmon with garlicky chickpeas

Add a mildly spicy twist to salmon with this satisfying and smart one-pot.

TAKES 25 MINUTES • SERVES 4

4 tbsp olive oil
2 garlic cloves, finely chopped
2 x 400g cans chickpeas, drained and rinsed
150ml/¼ pint vegetable or fish stock
4 skinless salmon fillets, about 150g/5oz each
2 tsp black peppercorns, roughly crushed
1 tsp paprika
zest and juice 2 limes, plus wedges to garnish
130g bag baby leaf spinach

1 Heat the oven to 190C/170C fan/gas 5. Heat 3 tablespoons oil in an ovenproof pan, add the garlic, then gently cook for around 5 minutes without browning. Add the chickpeas and stock. Sit the salmon fillets on top of the chickpeas, then scatter the fillets with the pepper, paprika, lime zest and some salt. Drizzle with the remaining oil. Bake for 12–15 minutes until the salmon is just cooked and the chickpeas are warmed right through.
2 Lift the salmon off and keep warm. Put the pan over a medium heat and lightly mash the chickpeas using a potato masher. Fold in the spinach leaves – they will quickly wilt. Season with lime juice and salt and pepper. Serve with the salmon, garnished with lime wedges.

PER SERVING 531 kcals, protein 41g, carbs 23g, fat 32g, sat fat 5g, fibre 6g, sugar 2g, salt 1.01g

Speedy meatball stew

Like many stews, the flavour of this meal in a bowl will actually improve if you make it ahead then reheat it.

TAKES 20 MINUTES • SERVES 4

2 medium potatoes, peeled and cut into bite-size cubes
1 tbsp olive oil
250g pack small lean beef meatballs
1 onion, chopped
2 garlic cloves, chopped
1 tbsp chopped fresh rosemary
560ml jar passata
200g/7oz frozen peas
few Parmesan shavings, to garnish (optional)
good crusty bread, to serve

1 Boil the potatoes for 10 minutes until they are tender.
2 Meanwhile, heat the oil in a large pan. Season the meatballs, then brown them all over for about 5 minutes. Remove from the pan, drain off any excess fat, then add the onion, garlic and rosemary. Fry gently for 5 minutes.
3 Add the passata to the pan, bring to a simmer, then add the meatballs. Simmer for 5 minutes or until everything is cooked through. Add the potatoes and peas, then simmer for 1 minute. Top with the Parmesan, if using, and eat with good crusty bread.

PER SERVING 286 kcals, protein 20g, carbs 28g, fat 11g, sat fat 4g, fibre 4g, sugar 9g, salt 1.68g

Pepper-crusted salmon with garlicky chickpeas

Speedy meatball stew

Bean and dill pilau with garlicky yogurt

Make the most of what's in your storecupboard and freezer with this easy throw-together rice dish.

TAKES 25 MINUTES • SERVES 2 (EASILY DOUBLED)

2 onions, halved and thinly sliced
25g/1oz butter
175g/6oz basmati rice
20g pack fresh dill, stalks and fronds chopped but kept separate
450ml/16fl oz vegetable stock mixed with a good pinch of saffron strands or ground turmeric
300g/10oz frozen mixed broad beans, peas and green beans
100g/3½oz Greek yogurt
1 tbsp milk
1 small garlic clove, crushed

1 Fry the onions in the butter for 5 minutes until golden. Add the rice and dill stalks then stir them around the pan.
2 Pour in the saffron or turmeric stock, bring to the boil, then cover and simmer for 5 minutes. Add the beans and half the dill fronds. Cook for 5 minutes more until the liquid has been absorbed into the rice.
3 Meanwhile, stir the yogurt, milk and garlic together with some seasoning. Spoon the yogurt on top of the rice, then sprinkle with the remaining dill.

PER SERVING 609 kcals, protein 20g, carbs 99g, fat 18g, sat fat 10g, fibre 10g, sugar 13g, salt 0.63g

Italian stuffed chicken

So simple you'll make this again and again. The tomatoes and the creamy filling not only taste great but also keep the chicken dry as it cooks.

TAKES 25 MINUTES • SERVES 4

2 tbsp chopped olives or sundried tomatoes
1 garlic clove, crushed
½ tsp dried mixed herbs
200g tub full-fat soft cheese (use a garlicky one, if you like)
4 plump skinless chicken breasts
4 ripe tomatoes, sliced
olive oil, for drizzling
green salad and crusty bread, to serve

1 Heat the oven to 220C/200C fan/gas 7. Beat the olives or sundried tomatoes, garlic and almost all the herbs into the cheese, then season. Cut a slit along the side of each chicken breast, then use a knife to open it out into a pocket.
2 Stuff each breast with a quarter of the cheese mix, then press to close. Lift on to a greased baking sheet. Season the top of the chicken, then overlap tomato slices over the top of each piece of chicken. Season, then scatter with the remaining herbs. Drizzle with olive oil.
3 Roast for 20 minutes until the chicken is golden around the edges and the tomatoes look a little shrivelled. Serve with a green salad and some crusty bread to mop up the juices.

PER SERVING 332 kcals, protein 37g, carbs 5g, fat 18g, sat fat 9g, fibre 1g, sugar 4g, salt 1.17g

Bean and dill pilau with garlicky yogurt

Italian stuffed chicken

Aubergine and mushroom curry

Here's a one-pan curry that both meat eaters and vegetarians will love. The texture of the aubergine plus the almonds in the creamy sauce makes it a really satisfying meat-free meal.

TAKES 30 MINUTES • SERVES 4

3 tbsp olive oil
2 aubergines, each cut into about 8 chunks
250g/9oz chestnut mushrooms, halved
20g bunch fresh coriander, stalks and leaves
    separated
2 large onions, quartered
thumb-size knob of ginger
3 garlic cloves, coarsely chopped
1 fat red chilli, deseeded and half roughly
    chopped
1 tbsp each ground cumin and coriander
1 tbsp tomato purée
450ml/16fl oz vegetable stock
5 tbsp ground almonds
200g/7oz full-fat natural yogurt

1 Heat 2 tablespoons oil in a large frying pan, then fry the aubergines for 10 minutes until golden and soft. (The chunks will absorb all the oil at first, but keep cooking and it will be released again.) Add the mushrooms after 5 minutes; once golden, tip them out of the pan.
2 Meanwhile, whizz the coriander stalks, onions, ginger, garlic and chopped chilli to a paste in a food processor. Add 1 tablespoon oil to the pan, then fry the paste for 2 minutes.
3 Tip in the spices and tomato purée. Stir for 2 minutes, then return the aubergines and mushrooms. Tip in the stock, ground almonds and most of the yogurt. Simmer for 5 minutes until the sauce has thickened. Serve with slices of the remaining chilli, coriander leaves and a drizzle of the remaining yogurt.

PER SERVING 307 kcals, protein 11g, carbs 20g, fat 21g, sat fat 3g, fibre 7g, sugar 14g, salt 0.32g

Fragrant pork and rice

Mild spices and a rich tomato sauce make so much more of sausages. The rice is cooked in the sauce and absorbs the tasty juices.

TAKES 40 MINUTES • SERVES 4

4–6 good-quality sausages
1 tbsp olive oil
½ onion, finely chopped
2 garlic cloves, crushed
2 tsp each ground cumin and coriander
140g/5oz long grain rice
850ml/1½ pints vegetable stock
400g can chopped tomatoes
½ small bunch of fresh coriander, leaves picked
crusty bread, to serve

1 Split the sausage skins, squeeze out the meat, then roll it into small meatballs, each about the size of a large olive. Heat the oil in a large non-stick pan, then brown the meatballs well on all sides until cooked – you might need to do this in batches. Set the meatballs aside.
2 Add the onion and garlic to the pan. Soften for 5 minutes, stir in the spices and rice, then cook for another minute. Pour in the stock and tomatoes. Bring to a simmer, scraping up any sausagey bits from the bottom of the pan. Simmer for 10 minutes until the rice is just cooked, then stir in the meatballs with some seasoning. Ladle into bowls, scatter with coriander and serve with crusty bread.

PER SERVING 408 kcals, protein 17g, carbs 43g, fat 20g, sat fat 5g, fibre 2g, sugar 6g, salt 1.56g

Fragrant pork and rice

Aubergine and mushroom curry

10-minute pad Thai

It's easy to make your own version of this classic Thai street food. Better still, this version is low in fat. Use raw prawns, if you can, as they'll add masses more flavour than ready-cooked ones.

TAKES 10 MINUTES • SERVES 2 (EASILY DOUBLED)

200g/7oz raw peeled prawns
1 small pack fresh coriander, stalks finely
    chopped, leaves roughly chopped
2 x 200g packs straight-to-wok pad Thai noodles
85g/3oz beansprouts
1 egg, beaten
juice 1 lime, plus wedges to serve
1 tbsp fish sauce
2 tsp sugar
1 tbsp roasted peanuts, roughly chopped,
    to serve

1 Dry-fry the prawns and coriander stalks in a non-stick frying pan for 1–2 minutes until the prawns are just pink. Add the noodles, beansprouts, egg, lime juice, fish sauce and sugar. Quickly toss together for 1 minute more until the egg is just cooked and everything is well mixed (you might want to use a pair of tongs to make this easier).
2 Remove from the heat, mix in most of the coriander leaves, then divide between two bowls. Scatter with the remaining coriander and the peanuts, and serve with lime wedges for squeezing over.

PER SERVING 494 kcals, protein 37g, carbs 69g, fat 10g, sat fat 2g, fibre 4g, sugar 9g, salt 2.91g

Pork and peanut noodles

All the flavours of pork satay come together in this delicious stir-fry. If your noodles look like they're sticking once drained, add a few drops of oil to the bowl (vegetable or sesame oil) and toss to coat.

TAKES 20 MINUTES • SERVES 4

300g/10oz thin rice noodles
500g pack minced pork
1 garlic clove, crushed
250g pack mangetout
3 tbsp crunchy peanut butter
1 red chilli, deseeded and finely chopped
2 tsp light muscovado sugar
1 tbsp light soy sauce
1 small bunch fresh coriander, chopped,
    to garnish

1 Place the noodles in a large bowl and cover with boiling water. Leave to soak for 5 minutes, then drain and set aside.
2 Meanwhile, heat a wok or large frying pan and cook the pork mince over a high heat for 10 minutes, or until the juices have evaporated and the pork is starting to look crisp. Throw in the garlic and mangetout, and fry together for 2 minutes.
3 Whisk together the peanut butter, chilli, sugar and soy sauce in a bowl, then loosen with 2 tablespoons warm water. Add the noodles and peanut sauce to the pan, toss everything well, then fry for 1 minute, stirring until warmed through. Sprinkle over the coriander and serve in bowls.

PER SERVING 551 kcals, protein 33g, carbs 68g, fat 18g, sat fat 6g, fibre 2g, sugar 6g, salt 1.02g

10-minute pad Thai

Pork and peanut noodles

Trout with almonds and red peppers

Trout is quick and easy to cook, and makes a great heart-healthy meal. Swap for salmon, if you like; the cooking time will be the same.

TAKES 40 MINUTES • SERVES 2

1 large red pepper, deseeded and chopped
2 large tomatoes, roughly chopped, or handful of cherry tomatoes, halved
1 garlic clove, chopped
1 tbsp olive oil, plus a little extra
1 tbsp balsamic vinegar
2 trout fillets, about 140g/5oz each
2 tbsp flaked almonds
lemon wedges and rocket leaves, to serve

1 Heat the oven to 190C/170C fan/gas 5. Tip the pepper, tomatoes, garlic, oil and vinegar into a roasting tin, then toss them together. Roast for 20 minutes, then make a space in the roasting tin for the trout fillets, scattering with the almonds and a little salt and pepper.
2 Return the tin to the oven for a further 10–15 minutes, until the fish is cooked and the almonds lightly toasted. Serve with lemon wedges for squeezing over and rocket on the side.

PER SERVING 326 kcals, protein 31g, carbs 11g, fat 18g, sat fat 3g, fibre 3g, sugar 11g, salt 0.24g

Spiced pork with stir-fried greens

Use a proper stir-fry oil, if you can, as it's infused with ginger, garlic and spices, giving an authentic flavour hit.

TAKES 20–30 MINUTES • SERVES 2 (EASILY DOUBLED)

1 tbsp stir-fry oil or vegetable oil
250g/9oz pork escalopes, sliced into thin strips
bunch of spring onions, trimmed and sliced
175g/6oz broccoli, broken into small bite-size florets
3 celery sticks, sliced
2 heads pak or bok choi, broken into separate leaves
2 tbsp chopped fresh coriander
finely grated zest and juice 1 lime
few thin slices of red chilli or dash of sweet chilli sauce

1 Heat the oil in a wok or large frying pan, add the pork and stir fry briskly for 3–4 minutes. Tip in the spring onions, broccoli and celery and stir fry over a high heat for 4 more minutes.
2 Add the pak or bok choi and cook for a minute or so until the leaves have wilted. Toss in the coriander and lime zest, squeeze in a little lime juice and add the chilli slices or sauce. Season with salt and pepper and serve straight away.

PER SERVING 260 kcals, protein 34g, carbs 5g, fat 12g, sat fat 2.3g, fibre 3.7g, added sugar none, salt 0.59g

Trout with almonds and red peppers

Spiced pork with stir-fried greens

Tortellini with pesto and broccoli

Do something different with your pasta and pesto – broccoli goes fantastically well with both and makes a pack of pasta go further. Eaten cold, it's a great lunchbox filler, too.

TAKES 10 MINUTES • SERVES 2 (EASILY DOUBLED)

140g/5oz Tenderstem or regular broccoli, cut into short lengths
250g pack fresh tortellini (ham and cheese works well)
3 tbsp fresh pesto
2 tbsp toasted pine nuts
1 tbsp balsamic vinegar
8 cherry tomatoes, halved

1 Bring a large pan of water to the boil. Add the broccoli, cook for 2 minutes, then add the tortellini and cook for 2 minutes, or according to the packet instructions.
2 Drain everything, gently rinse under cold water until cool, then tip into a bowl. Toss with the pesto, pine nuts and balsamic vinegar. Add the tomatoes. Serve warm or at room temperature.

PER SERVING 573 kcals, protein 24g, carbs 64g, fat 26g, sat fat 9g, fibre 5g, sugar 8g, salt 1.58g

Sticky green stir-fry with beef

Low in fat, high in iron and vitamin C, and including three of your 5-a-day, this is just about the perfect healthy stir-fry.

TAKES 20 MINUTES • SERVES 4

1 tbsp sunflower oil
2 x 200g/7oz sirloin steaks, trimmed of fat and thinly sliced
1 broccoli head, cut into small florets
2 garlic cloves, sliced
300g/10oz sugar snap peas
4 spring onions, thickly sliced
3 pak choi, leaves separated and cut into quarters
4 tbsp hoisin sauce

1 Heat the oil in a large wok or deep frying pan, then sizzle the beef strips for 3–4 minutes until browned. Remove and set aside. Toss the broccoli and garlic into the wok with a splash of water, then fry over a high heat for 4–5 minutes until starting to soften.
2 Add the peas, spring onions and pak choi, then stir-fry for another 2–3 minutes, then stir in the hoisin sauce and beef. Heat through quickly, adding a splash of water if it seems a little dry. Great with noodles or rice.

PER SERVING 245 kcals, protein 31g, carbs 12g, fat 9g, sat fat 2g, fibre 4g, sugar 10g, salt 0.8g

Beans and bangers

If your family goes mad for sausages, put this in the middle of the table and watch them dive in. The beans make a healthy and convenient change to potatoes.

TAKES 40 MINUTES • SERVES 4

1 tbsp olive oil
8 good-quality pork sausages (Toulouse or Sicilian varieties work well)
2 carrots, halved then sliced
2 onions, finely chopped
2 tbsp red wine vinegar
2 x 410g cans mixed beans in water, drained and rinsed
400ml/14fl oz chicken stock
100g/3½oz frozen peas
2 tbsp Dijon mustard

1 Heat the oil in a large pan. Sizzle the sausages for about 6 minutes, turning occasionally, until brown on all sides. Remove to a plate. Tip the carrots and onions into the pan and cook for 8 minutes, stirring occasionally, until the onions are soft. Add the vinegar to the pan, then stir in the drained beans. Pour over the stock, nestle the sausages in with the beans, then simmer everything for 10 minutes.
2 Scatter in the frozen peas, cook for 2 minutes more until heated through, then take off the heat and stir in the mustard. Season to taste. Serve scooped straight from the pan.

PER SERVING 569 kcals, protein 35g, carbs 41g, fat 31g, sat fat 9g, fibre 11g, sugar 13g, salt 2.81g

Leek, butter bean and chorizo gratin

Use up slightly stale bread to make the crunchy topping for this easy bake. Just a little chorizo goes a long way, keeping the dish low in fat but with a big, gutsy flavour.

TAKES 35 MINUTES • SERVES 4

1 tbsp olive oil
75g pack chorizo, roughly chopped
4 large leeks, thinly sliced
3 garlic cloves, sliced
100ml/3½fl oz dry sherry
2 x 400g cans butter beans, drained and rinsed
450ml/16fl oz hot vegetable stock
85g/3oz bread, torn into pieces

1 Heat the oven to 200C/180C fan/gas 6. Pour the oil into a baking dish, toss with the chorizo, leeks and half the garlic then bake uncovered for 10 minutes. Stir in the sherry, beans and stock, and return to the oven for 5 minutes. Season.
2 Meanwhile, blitz the bread to coarse crumbs with the remaining garlic. Scatter this over the chorizo, leek and bean mix, and bake for 10 minutes more until golden.

PER SERVING 275 kcals, protein 15g, carbs 32g, fat 9g, sat fat 2g, fibre 9g, sugar 7g, salt 2.41g

Spring chicken in a pot, page 46

Meat and poultry

Smoky maple duck salad

The smoky chipotle chilli paste in this recipe can easily be swapped for harissa paste. Either way, it's a one-pan winner.

TAKES 30 MINUTES • SERVES 2 (EASILY DOUBLED)

2 duck breasts, skin on and slashed
3 tbsp maple syrup
1 garlic clove, crushed
1 tbsp chipotle chilli paste
160g bag bistro salad
1 bunch radishes, about 200g/7oz, thinly
    sliced or grated
1 tbsp sherry vinegar

1 Heat the oven to 220C/200C fan/gas 7. Place a roasting tin in the oven for 5 minutes. Season the duck well, then carefully put into the hot tin, skin-side down. Roast for 10 minutes until the skin is golden and crisp, and the fat has run out. (Or leave for 15 minutes if you prefer well done.)
2 Meanwhile, mix 2 tablespoons of the maple syrup with the garlic and chilli paste. Tip the fat out of the pan, turn the duck over, then roast for 5 minutes, basting with the maple mix once or twice until glazed and sticky. Remove and let the duck rest for 5 minutes.
3 Pile the salad and the radishes on to plates. Slice the duck; nestle it into the salad. Stir the rest of the maple syrup and the sherry vinegar into the pan juices, then drizzle over the salad to serve.

PER SERVING 527 kcals, protein 32g, carbs 20g, fat 36g, sat fat 10g, fibre 2g, sugar 18g, salt 0.54g

Fully loaded Cajun chicken burgers

Stack up the flavours in these big and bold chicken burgers.

TAKES 35 MINUTES • SERVES 4

1 tbsp ground cumin
1 tbsp ground coriander
1 tbsp paprika
2 tbsp olive oil
4 skinless chicken breasts, flattened a little
4 ciabatta rolls, split
4 rashers smoked bacon
2 avocados
mayonnaise, to spread (optional)
4 small handfuls baby leaf spinach

1 Mix together the spices in a large dish with some salt and pepper and 1 tablespoon of the oil. Coat the chicken in the mix.
2 Heat a large frying pan, then toast the cut sides of the buns in the pan. Set aside. Heat the remaining oil in the pan then sizzle the chicken for 5 minutes on each side. Push to one side of the pan, then fry the bacon for a few minutes until cooked.
3 While the chicken is cooking, slice the avocados. To assemble the burgers, spread the buns with mayonnaise, if using, top with handful of spinach, then a rasher of bacon. To keep the avocado in place, slice the chicken and place the avocado between the chicken slices. Top with the bun lid, press down lightly and serve.

PER SERVING 721 kcals, protein 51g, carbs 51g, fat 36g, sat fat 10g, fibre 5g, sugar 2g, salt 2.84g

Smoky maple duck salad

Fully loaded Cajun chicken burgers

Crispy-skin chicken thighs

You can leave the chicken to marinate in the fridge for up to a day, if you like.

TAKES 45–55 MINUTES • SERVES 4

8 plump chicken thighs, skin on
2 lemons
2 tbsp chopped fresh tarragon
2 tbsp olive oil
750g/1lb 10oz new potatoes, scrubbed and
    cut into wedges
2 tsp paprika, sweet or smoked
green salad, to serve

1 Heat the oven to 220C/200C fan/gas 7. Slash the skin of each chicken thigh three times. Finely grate the zest from 1 lemon and squeeze the juice from both. Mix in a shallow dish with the tarragon, 1 tablespoon of the oil and some salt and pepper. Add the chicken and turn to coat in the marinade.
2 Spread the potato wedges over the base of a roasting tin. Toss in the remaining oil and sprinkle with paprika. Set a rack on top and arrange the chicken pieces on the rack. Roast for 30–40 minutes until the chicken is well browned and the potatoes are tender. Serve hot with a simple green salad.

PER SERVING 917 kcals, protein 64g, carbs 32g, fat 60g, sat fat 17g, fibre 2g, added sugar none, salt 0.74g

Lighter lamb burgers with smoky oven chips

The combination of lean lamb, couscous and carrot makes these burgers both nutritionally balanced and so satisfying.

TAKES 50 MINUTES • SERVES 4

100g/3½oz couscous
2 carrots, finely grated
250g pack extra-lean minced lamb
1 bunch spring onions,
    finely chopped
1 bunch fresh mint, finely chopped
1 egg, beaten
rocket leaves and raita or natural
    yogurt, to garnish

FOR THE SMOKY OVEN CHIPS
1 tbsp olive oil
750g/1lb 10oz sweet potatoes,
    peeled and cut into chips
1–2 tsp smoked paprika

1 Heat the oven to 200C/180C fan/gas 6. Place the couscous in a heatproof bowl and pour over 100ml/3½fl oz boiling water. Leave for a couple of minutes until all the liquid has been absorbed. Squeeze any liquid out of the carrots, then stir into the couscous along with the mince, spring onions, mint and egg. Season well and shape into four large burgers.
2 Pour the oil into a large, shallow non-stick baking sheet and heat in the oven. Add the sweet potato chips, stir around until coated with oil, then roast for 35 minutes.
3 After 15 minutes, add the burgers to the sheet. Ten minutes after this, sprinkle the paprika over the chips, shake to coat, then roast for 10 minutes more until the chips and the burgers are cooked through. Serve with the rocket and a dollop of the raita or yogurt.

PER SERVING 400 kcals, protein 19g, carbs 58g, fat 12g, sat fat 4g, fibre 6g, sugar 15g, salt 0.28g

Lighter lamb burgers with smoky oven chips

Crispy-skin chicken thighs

Chicken with creamy bacon penne

This amazingly quick and tasty dish works well with fresh salmon, too. Just cook for 3 minutes on each side and leave out the bacon.

TAKES 10 MINUTES • SERVES 2

1 tbsp olive oil
2 boneless, skinless chicken breasts
100g/3½oz smoked lardons (chopped bacon)
4 tbsp dry white wine
100g/3½oz frozen petits pois
5 tbsp double cream
220g pack 'instant' cooked penne

1 Heat the oil in a deep non-stick frying pan, add the chicken breasts and scatter with the lardons. Leave to cook over a high heat for 4 minutes while you gather the other ingredients together.
2 Turn the chicken over in the pan, give the lardons a stir, then pour in the wine and let it bubble over a high heat until it has virtually evaporated. Now add the peas, cream and penne, season and stir well. Cover the pan and cook for 4 minutes more until the chicken is cooked all the way through. Serve straight away.

PER SERVING 639 kcals, protein 48g, carbs 24g, fat 38g, sat fat 17g, fibre 3g, added sugar none, salt 1.86g

Summer pork and potatoes

A great dish for everyone to help themselves from. A green salad, dressed lightly with olive oil and lemon juice, is all you need to go with it.

TAKES 1¼–1½ HOURS • SERVES 4

olive oil, for drizzling
750g/1lb 10oz new potatoes, scrubbed and sliced
500g/1lb 2oz vine-ripened tomatoes, sliced
leaves of 3–4 rosemary sprigs, finely chopped
2 garlic cloves, chopped
4 pork chops or steaks
green salad, to serve

1 Heat the oven to 200C/180C fan/gas 6. Drizzle a little olive oil over the base of a shallow ovenproof dish that is wide enough to take the chops in one layer. Arrange rows of potatoes and tomatoes across the dish, seasoning with salt and pepper as you go and sprinkling with half the rosemary and all the garlic.
2 Drizzle a couple more tablespoons of olive oil over the vegetables and bake for 30 minutes, then sit the pork on top, season and sprinkle with the remaining rosemary. Return to the oven for 35–45 minutes, until the pork and potatoes are tender. Serve with a green salad.

PER SERVING 527 kcals, protein 25g, carbs 35g, fat 33g, sat fat 11g, fibre 3g, added sugar none, salt 0.2g

Chicken with creamy bacon penne

Summer pork and potatoes

Italian chicken and butternut pie

This one-pot recipe has an Italian theme running through it with the wine, pancetta and plum tomatoes. Although this is a pie, you don't have to make any pastry – there's not a rolling pin in sight!

TAKES 1¼–1½ HOURS • SERVES 6

3 tbsp olive oil
8 large skinless chicken thigh fillets, quartered
130g pack cubed pancetta
1 large butternut squash, flesh cut into
   2.5cm/1in cubes
1 large onion, thinly sliced
2 garlic cloves, thinly sliced
1 tsp dried marjoram
200ml/7fl oz Italian red wine
1 level tbsp plain flour
2 x 400g cans Italian plum tomatoes
2 tbsp redcurrant or cranberry jelly
1 garlic and herb or plain
   ciabatta, very thinly sliced
3 tbsp freshly grated Parmesan

1 Heat 2 tablespoons oil in a large casserole and lightly brown the chicken all over. Lift out of the pan, tip in the pancetta, squash and onion, and soften for 8 minutes, stirring occasionally. Return the chicken to the pan, add the garlic and marjoram and cook for 1 minute. Pour all but 2 tablespoons of the wine into the pan and bubble for 5 minutes.
2 Blend the flour with reserved wine until smooth. Stir into the pan with the tomatoes, jelly and seasoning. Lower the heat, half-cover, then simmer for 30–40 minutes until the squash is tender.
3 Heat the oven to 220C/200C fan/gas 7. Lay the slices of ciabatta on top of the casserole, drizzle with the remaining olive oil, sprinkle with the Parmesan and some black pepper. Bake for 15 minutes or until golden.

PER SERVING 491 kcals, protein 41g, carbs 42g, fat 16g, sat fat 5g, fibre 4g, added sugar 2g, salt 2.17g

Spring chicken in a pot

Chicken thighs cook to melting softness and inject plenty of flavour into the stock in this vibrant and healthy herby casserole. They are also easier on the purse than breast meat.

TAKES ABOUT 1 HOUR • SERVES 4

1 tbsp olive oil
1 onion, chopped
500g/1lb 2oz boneless skinless chicken thighs
300g/10oz small new potatoes
425ml/¾ pint low-salt vegetable stock
350g/12oz broccoli, cut into small florets
350g/12oz spring greens, shredded
140g/5oz petits pois
1 bunch spring onions, sliced
2 tbsp pesto

1 Heat the oil in a large, heavy pan. Add the onion, gently fry for 5 minutes until softened, add the chicken, then fry until lightly coloured. Add the potatoes, stock and plenty of freshly ground black pepper, then bring to the boil. Cover, then simmer for 30 minutes until the potatoes are tender and the chicken is cooked through.
2 Add the broccoli, spring greens, petits pois and spring onions, stir well, then return to the boil. Cover, then cook for 5 minutes more, stir in the pesto and serve.

PER SERVING 339 kcals, protein 36g, carbs 27g, fat 10g, sat fat 3g, fibre 8g, sugar 12g, salt 0.5g

Chicken and white bean stew

This freezes really well, so why not make double and freeze half for next time?

TAKES 1 HOUR 20 MINUTES • SERVES 4

2 tbsp sunflower oil
400g/14oz boneless skinless chicken thighs,
    cut into chunks
1 onion, finely chopped
3 carrots, finely chopped
3 celery sticks, finely chopped
2 fresh thyme sprigs or ½ tsp dried
1 bay leaf, fresh or dried
600ml/1 pint vegetable or chicken stock
2 x 400g cans haricot beans, drained and
    rinsed
a little chopped fresh parsley
crusty bread, to serve

1 Heat the oil in a large pan, add the chicken, then fry until lightly browned. Add the veg, then fry for a few minutes more. Stir in the herbs and stock. Bring to the boil. Stir well, reduce the heat, then cover and cook for 40 minutes, until the chicken is tender.
2 Stir the beans into the pan, then simmer for 5 minutes. Season to taste, stir in the parsley and serve with crusty bread.

PER SERVING 291 kcals, protein 30g, carbs 24g, fat 9g, sat fat 2g, fibre 11g, sugar 9g, salt 0.66g

Chicken and thyme bake

Try Taleggio, ripe Brie or dolcelatte if you don't like goat's cheese.

TAKES 35–40 MINUTES • SERVES 4

4 part-boned chicken breasts
140g/5oz firm goat's cheese, sliced
bunch of fresh thyme
500g pack cherry tomatoes
olive oil, for drizzling
splash of dry white wine
French bread or ready-cooked saffron rice,
    to serve

1 Heat the oven to 190C/170C fan/gas 5. Loosen the skin from the chicken breasts and stuff with the slices of goat's cheese and a sprig of thyme. Put in a shallow ovenproof dish.
2 Halve the cherry tomatoes and scatter around the chicken with a few more sprigs of thyme, a drizzle of olive oil and splash of white wine. Season with pepper, and salt if you wish.
3 Bake for 25–30 minutes until the chicken is tender and golden. Serve with crusty French bread to mop up the juices or some saffron rice.

PER SERVING 330 kcals, protein 40g, carbs 5g, fat 16g, sat fat 8g, fibre 1g, added sugar none, salt 1.24g

Flambéed chicken with asparagus

An elegant one-pan spring dish that looks and tastes very special.

TAKES 45 MINUTES • SERVES 4

4 skinless chicken breasts
1 tbsp seasoned plain flour
2 tbsp olive oil
knob of butter
4 shallots, finely chopped
4 tbsp brandy or Cognac
300ml/½ pint chicken stock
16 asparagus spears, halved
4 rounded tbsp crème fraîche
1 tbsp chopped fresh tarragon
boiled new potatoes, to serve

1 Dust the chicken with the flour. Heat the oil and butter in a large, wide pan with a lid, add the chicken, then fry on all sides until nicely browned. Add the shallots, then fry for about 2 minutes until they start to soften, but not colour. Pour in the brandy, carefully ignite, then stand well back until the flames have died down. Stir in the stock and bring to the boil. Reduce the heat, cover, then cook for 15 minutes until the chicken is just tender.
2 Add the asparagus to the sauce. Cover, then cook for 5 minutes more until tender. Stir in the crème fraîche and tarragon, and warm through. Season to taste and serve with boiled new potatoes.

PER SERVING 395 kcals, protein 42g, carbs 7g, fat 19g, sat fat 8g, fibre 3g, sugar 4g, salt 0.9g

Creamy pesto chicken with roasted tomatoes

This is pure summer in a pan; simple to make and bursting with fresh Italian flavours.

TAKES 35 MINUTES • SERVES 4

4 skinless chicken breasts
3 tbsp pesto
85g/3oz mascarpone
4 tbsp olive oil
100g/3½oz fresh breadcrumbs (preferably from day-old bread)
175g/6oz cherry tomatoes on the vine
handful of pine nuts
handful of fresh basil leaves, to garnish
crusty bread, to serve

1 Heat the oven to 200C/180C fan/gas 6. Use a small sharp knife to make a slit along the side of each chicken breast to form a pocket. Mix together the pesto and mascarpone, then carefully spoon a quarter of the mixture into each chicken breast and smooth over the opening to seal.
2 Brush a little oil, about 1 teaspoon, all over each chicken breast and season well. Tip the breadcrumbs on to a plate and season. Press each breast into the crumbs to coat. Place in a lightly oiled, shallow baking dish along with the tomatoes. Drizzle over the remaining oil.
3 Roast for 20–25 minutes until the chicken is golden and cooked through. Scatter over the pine nuts and cook for 2 minutes more. Sprinkle with basil leaves and serve with crusty bread.

PER SERVING 545 kcals, protein 40g, carbs 22g, fat 33g, sat fat 10g, fibre 1g, sugar 3g, salt 0.82g

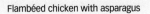
Flambéed chicken with asparagus

Creamy pesto chicken with roasted tomatoes

Rosemary chicken with tomato sauce

Anchovies are often used in Italian cooking to add a deeply savoury edge to a recipe. This is a great dish for the freezer.

TAKES 35 MINUTES • SERVES 4

1 tbsp olive oil
8 boneless skinless chicken thighs
1 fresh rosemary sprig, leaves finely chopped
1 red onion, finely sliced
3 garlic cloves, sliced
2 anchovy fillets, chopped
400g can chopped tomatoes
1 tbsp capers, drained
75ml/2½fl oz red wine, water or chicken
   stock
crusty bread, to serve

1 Heat half the oil in a non-stick pan, then brown the chicken all over. Add half the chopped rosemary, stir to coat, then set aside on a plate.
2 In the same pan, heat the rest of the oil, then gently fry the onion for roughly 5 minutes until soft. Add the garlic, anchovies and remaining rosemary, then fry for a few minutes more until fragrant. Pour in the tomatoes and capers with the wine, water or stock.
3 Bring to the boil, then return the chicken pieces to the pan. Cover, then cook for 20 minutes until the chicken is tender. Season and serve with crusty bread.

PER SERVING 275 kcals, protein 44g, carbs 5g, fat 9g, sat fat 3g, fibre 2g, sugar 4g, salt 1.09g

Sausages with oregano, mushrooms and olives

Enjoy sausages without worrying about their fat content with this quick, full of flavour casserole.

TAKES 30 MINUTES • SERVES 4

450g pack reduced-fat sausages
1 tsp sunflower oil
2 tsp dried oregano
2 garlic cloves, sliced
400g can cherry or chopped tomatoes
200ml/7fl oz beef stock
100g/3½oz pitted black olives
500g pack mushrooms, thickly sliced

1 Using kitchen scissors, snip the sausages into meatball-size pieces. Heat a large pan and fry the pieces in the oil for about 5 minutes until golden all over.
2 Add the oregano and garlic, fry for 1 minute more, then tip in the tomatoes, stock, olives and mushrooms. Simmer for 15 minutes until the sausages are cooked through and the sauce has reduced a little.

PER SERVING 264 kcals, protein 20g, carbs 12g, fat 16g, sat fat 4g, fibre 4g, sugar 4g, salt 2.19g

Rosemary chicken with tomato sauce

Sausages with oregano, mushrooms and olives

Chicken and spring vegetable stew

A fresh and delicious dish that's good enough to eat every day.

TAKES 25–30 MINUTES • SERVES 2

2 chicken breasts, skin on
1 tbsp olive oil
200g/7oz baby new potatoes, scrubbed and
    thinly sliced
500ml/18fl oz chicken stock
200g pack mixed spring vegetables (broccoli,
    peas, broad beans and sliced courgette)
2 tbsp crème fraîche
handful of fresh tarragon leaves, roughly
    chopped, or ½ tsp dried tarragon

1 Fry the chicken in the olive oil in a wide pan for 5 minutes on each side. Throw in the potatoes and stir to coat. Pour over the chicken stock, cover and simmer for 10 minutes until the potatoes are almost cooked through.
2 Remove the lid and turn the heat to high. Boil the stock down until it just coats the bottom of the pan. Scatter the vegetables into the pan, cover again and cook for about 3 minutes.
3 Stir in the crème fraîche to make a creamy sauce, season with salt and pepper to taste, then add the tarragon. Serve straight from the pan.

PER SERVING 386 kcals, protein 38g, carbs 23g, fat 16g, sat fat 6g, fibre 3g, added sugar none, salt 1.5g

Roast chicken and root vegetables

Transform your chicken breasts into something special. As a bonus, this dish is crammed with health-boosting vegetables.

TAKES 1¼–1½ HOURS • SERVES 4

1 small celeriac, peeled and cut into 2.5cm/1in
    chunks
400g/14oz swede, peeled and cut into 2.5cm/1in
    chunks
2 large sweet potatoes, scrubbed and cut into
    2.5cm/1in chunks
2 medium parsnips, scrubbed and quartered
    lengthways
2 large garlic cloves, thinly sliced
2 tbsp olive oil
½ tsp cumin seeds
a few sage leaves
4 boneless, skinless chicken breasts, about
    140g/5oz each
4 slices prosciutto

1 Heat the oven to 200C/180C fan/gas 6. Put the celeriac, swede, sweet potato, parsnips and garlic in a large roasting pan. Sprinkle with olive oil and cumin, and season with salt and pepper. Toss the vegetables together so they are lightly coated in oil. Put in the oven towards the top and roast for 30 minutes.
2 Meanwhile, lay a couple of sage leaves on each chicken breast, then wrap each with a slice of prosciutto to enclose.
3 Take the roasting tin from the oven and turn the vegetables over. Now lay the chicken on top. Roast for 30–35 minutes more, until the vegetables are tender and the chicken is done.

PER SERVING 420 kcals, protein 43g, carbs 39g, fat 12g, sat fat 2g, fibre 12g, added sugar none, salt 1.11g

Chicken and spring vegetable stew

Roast chicken and root vegetables

Curry in a hurry

Look out for jars of ready-chopped ginger and chillies, and pouches of gujarati masala, in larger supermarkets.

TAKES 15 MINUTES • SERVES 2 (EASILY DOUBLED)

1 tbsp sunflower oil
1 red onion, thinly sliced
1 garlic clove
2 tsp ready-prepared ginger from a jar
½–1 tsp ready-chopped chillies from a jar
200g can chopped tomatoes
250g/9oz boneless, skinless chicken breasts, chopped
2tsp gujarati masala or garam masala
3 tbsp low-fat yogurt
handful of coriander leaves, roughly chopped or torn
garlic and coriander naan bread, to serve

1 Heat the oil in a pan, add the onion and fry until coloured. Crush the garlic into the pan, add the ginger and chillies and cook briefly. Add the tomatoes and a quarter of a can of water and bring to the boil. Simmer for 2 minutes, add the chicken and masala, cover and cook for 5–6 minutes.
2 Reduce the heat to a simmer, then stir in the yogurt, a tablespoon at a time. Sprinkle with coriander and serve with warm garlic and coriander naans.

PER SERVING 252 kcals, protein 34g, carbs 11g, fat 8g, sat fat 1.3g, fibre 1.8g, added sugar none, salt 0.46g

Spiced pineapple pork

The classic combination of pork and pineapple lives on in this slightly retro and irresistible sweet and sour one-pan dish.

TAKES 20 MINUTES • SERVES 4

2 tsp vegetable oil
4 pork steaks, trimmed of excess fat
2 tbsp light muscovado sugar
1 tbsp dark soy sauce
1 tsp tomato purée
432g can pineapple rings in juice, drained but juice reserved
½ tsp chilli powder
1 tsp Chinese five spice powder
coriander leaves, to garnish

1 Add the oil to a large non-stick pan, season the steaks well, then fry for 5 minutes on each side until golden and almost cooked through. Mix together the sugar, soy sauce, tomato purée and most of the pineapple juice in a bowl.
2 Add the pineapple rings to the pan and let them caramelise a little alongside the pork. Add the chilli and five spice to the pan, then fry for 1 minute until aromatic. Tip in the soy mix and let it bubble around the pork and pineapple for a few minutes until slightly reduced and sticky. Sprinkle with coriander before serving.

PER SERVING 315 kcals, protein 39g, carbs 22g, fat 9g, sat fat 3g, fibre 1g, sugar 21g, salt 1.25g

Massaman curry roast chicken

This full-flavoured chicken would make a great one-pan alternative to your usual weekend roast. Massaman curry paste is mild, so it's ideal for all the family.

TAKES 1 HOUR 40 MINUTES • SERVES 4

1 whole chicken, about 1.8kg/4lb
2 thumb-size knobs of ginger,
    1 roughly chopped, 1 grated
1 lemongrass stick, bashed with a rolling pin
1 lime, cut into quarters
70g pack Massaman curry paste
1 tsp olive oil
450g/1lb baby new potatoes, any larger ones
    halved
400ml can coconut milk
1 tsp brown sugar (any type)
200g/7oz green beans, trimmed
1 tsp fish sauce
2 tbsp unsalted peanuts, crushed, to scatter

1 Heat the oven to 200C/180C fan/gas 6. Put the chicken in a medium roasting tin. Stuff the chopped ginger, lemongrass and half the lime into the cavity. Tie the legs together with string. Mix 1 teaspoon of curry paste with the oil, rub all over the chicken, then season.
2 Cover the chicken loosely with foil, then roast for 35 minutes. Uncover, add the potatoes and stir them around in any juices. Roast for 40 minutes more or until the chicken is cooked through and golden and the potatoes tender. Rest the chicken, loosely covered.
3 Meanwhile, add the remaining curry paste and the grated ginger to a pan and fry for 2 minutes. Stir in the coconut milk and sugar, and boil for 5 minutes until slightly thickened.
4 Tip in the beans. Simmer for 4 minutes, splash in the fish sauce, resting juices and a squeeze of lime and scatter with peanuts.

PER SERVING 895 kcals, protein 61g, carbs 25g, fat 62g, sat fat 27g, fibre 2g, sugar 7g, salt 1.75g

Spiced chicken balti

If you haven't yet tried quinoa, give this a go. It's a filling grain that's super-good for you and cooks in the sauce just like rice would in a pilau.

TAKES 35 MINUTES • SERVES 4

1 tbsp sunflower oil
2 large onions, thickly sliced
4 skinless chicken breasts
4 tbsp balti paste
200g/7oz quinoa
400g can chopped tomatoes
1 litre/1¾ pints chicken stock
50g/2oz roasted salted cashews
1 small bunch fresh coriander, leaves chopped

1 Heat the oil in a large pan, fry the onions for 5 minutes until golden and softened, then tip out on to a plate. Add the chicken breasts to the pan, browning them for a few minutes on each side, then stir in the balti paste, quinoa and onions. Sizzle for a few minutes, then pour in the tomatoes and stock, and give everything a good mix. Bubble for 25 minutes until the quinoa is tender and saucy.
2 Stir in the cashews and most of the coriander with some seasoning, then scatter over the rest of the coriander to serve.

PER SERVING 527 kcals, protein 47g, carbs 45g, fat 19g, sat fat 3g, fibre 5g, sugar 14g, salt 1.83g

Chicken and couscous one-pot

If you like the zesty, spicy flavours of Moroccan food, you'll enjoy this simple-to-make chicken dish. The couscous absorbs all the cooking juices, keeping in every bit of flavour.

TAKES 1 HOUR 10 MINUTES • SERVES 4

8 chicken thighs, skin on and bone in
2 tsp ground turmeric
1 tbsp garam masala
2 tbsp sunflower oil
2 onions, finely sliced
3 garlic cloves, sliced
450ml/16fl oz chicken stock
a large handful of whole green olives
zest and juice 1 lemon
250g/9oz couscous
1 small bunch flat-leaf parsley, chopped

1 Toss the chicken thighs in half the spices and a pinch of salt. Heat 1 tablespoon of the oil in a large pan. Fry the chicken, skin-side down, for 10 minutes, then turn and cook for 2 minutes more. Remove from the pan. Add the remaining oil then gently fry the onions and garlic for 8 minutes until golden. Stir in remaining spices for 1 minute. Add the stock, olives and chicken to the pan, skin-side up.
2 Cover, then simmer for 40 minutes. Lift the chicken on to a plate and keep warm. Off the heat, stir the lemon juice and couscous into the pan – add boiling water just to cover the couscous, if needed. Re-cover then let stand for 5 minutes until the couscous is soft. Fork half the parsley and lemon zest through the couscous, then sit the chicken on top. Scatter with the remaining parsley and zest.

PER SERVING 900 kcals, protein 60g, carbs 42g, fat 56g, sat fat 15g, fibre 2g, sugar 5g, salt 1.75g

Chicken with harissa and tomatoes

Big on flavour, easy on effort, this spicy chicken is just the thing for a busy weeknight supper.

TAKES ABOUT 20 MINUTES • SERVES 4

4 skinless chicken breasts
2 tsp harissa paste
1 tsp olive oil
1 tsp dried oregano
250g pack cherry tomatoes
handful of pitted olives

1 Heat the oven to 200C/180C fan/gas 6. Put the chicken into a medium roasting tin, then rub with the harissa, oil and oregano. Cover with foil and roast for 5 minutes.
2 Remove the foil and add the cherry tomatoes and olives to the tin. Roast for 10 minutes more until the tomato skins start to split and the chicken is cooked through.

PER SERVING 184 kcals, protein 34g, carbs 2g, fat 4g, sat fat 1g, fibre 1g, sugar 2g, salt 0.41g

Chicken with harissa and tomatoes

Chicken and couscous one-pot

Moroccan lemon chicken

Try using a whole preserved lemon from a jar instead of half a lemon.

TAKES 40–45 MINUTES • SERVES 4

1kg pack boneless, skinless chicken thigh fillets
1 onion, chopped
3 garlic cloves, crushed
1 tbsp pilau rice seasoning
2 tbsp olive oil
½ lemon, finely chopped – the zest, pith and
  flesh
100g pack whole blanched almonds
140g/5oz green olives (the ones with stones in
  taste best)
250ml/9fl oz chicken stock
large handful of coriander or flat-leaf parsley,
  chopped

1 Toss the chicken with the onion, garlic, rice seasoning and oil in a microwave dish. Microwave on High for 8 minutes until everything is beginning to sizzle and the chicken is starting to change colour.
2 Toss the lemon, almonds and olives over the chicken. Pour in the stock and stir, keeping the chicken in a single layer.
3 Cover the dish with cling film, pierce a few times to allow the steam to escape, then return to the microwave for another 20 minutes until the liquid is bubbling vigorously and the chicken is cooked. Leave to stand for a few minutes before stirring in the coriander or parsley, then serve.

PER SERVING 488 kcals, protein 49g, carbs 8g, fat 29g, sat fat 5g, fibre 3g, added sugar none, salt 2.68g

Turkish lamb pilau

Fantastic textures and wonderful smells make this a very popular dish. You can use chicken and chicken stock, if you prefer.

TAKES 25–30 MINUTES • SERVES 4

small handful of pine nuts or flaked almonds
1 tbsp olive oil
1 large onion, halved and sliced
2 cinnamon sticks, broken in half
500g/1lb 2oz lean fillet or leg of lamb, cubed
250g/9oz basmati rice
1 lamb or vegetable stock cube
12 ready-to-eat dried apricots
handful of fresh mint leaves, roughly chopped

1 Dry fry the pine nuts or almonds in a large pan until lightly toasted, then tip on to a plate and set aside. Add the oil to the pan, then fry the onion and cinnamon together until starting to turn golden. Turn up the heat, stir in the lamb, fry until the meat changes colour, then tip in the rice and cook for 1 minute, stirring all the time.
2 Pour in 500ml/18fl oz boiling water, crumble in the stock cube, add the apricots, then season to taste. Turn the heat down, cover and simmer for 12 minutes until the rice is tender and the stock has been absorbed. Toss in the pine nuts or almonds and mint and serve.

PER SERVING 584 kcals, protein 32g, carbs 65g, fat 24g, sat fat 9g, fibre 3g, added sugar none, salt 1.4g

Moroccan lemon chicken

Turkish lamb pilau

One-pan rogan josh

Rich, tomatoey and better than anything you can buy – a homemade rogan josh is just three simple steps away. For a rich beef curry, use chunks of braising steak instead.

TAKES 1 HOUR 40 MINUTES • SERVES 6

2 onions, quartered
4 tbsp sunflower oil
4 garlic cloves, finely crushed
a thumb-size knob of ginger, peeled and
    very finely grated
2 tbsp Madras curry paste
2 tsp paprika
1 cinnamon stick
6 green cardamoms, bashed to break the
    shells
4 cloves
2 bay leaves
1 tbsp tomato purée
1kg/2lb 4oz lean leg of lamb, cut into
    generous cubes
150g/5oz Greek yogurt
chopped fresh coriander leaves, to serve

1 Put the onions in a food processor and whizz until very finely chopped. Heat the oil in a large heavy-based pan, then gently fry the onion with the lid on, stirring every now and then, until it is really golden and soft. Add the garlic and ginger, then fry for 5 minutes more.
2 Tip the curry paste, all the spices, bay leaves and tomato purée into the pan. Stir well over the heat for about 30 seconds, then add the meat and 300ml/½ pint water. Stir to mix, turn down the heat, then add the yogurt.
3 Cover the pan, then gently simmer for 40 minutes–1 hour until the meat is tender and the sauce nice and thick. Serve scattered with coriander.

PER SERVING 386 kcals, protein 37g, carbs 6g, fat 24g, sat fat 9g, fibre 1g, sugar 3g, salt 0.54g

Chicken biryani

It's so easy to recreate this classic Indian dish that you'll never order a takeaway again.

TAKES 50–60 MINUTES • SERVES 6

2 tbsp vegetable oil
6 large chicken thighs, skin on
1 large onion, finely sliced
2 tbsp curry powder (hot if you like it, mild for
    tamer curries)
350g/12oz easy-cook long grain rice
700ml/1½ pints chicken or vegetable stock
250g/9oz frozen peas

1 Heat the oven to 200C/180C fan/gas 6. Heat the oil in a large pan and fry the chicken thighs, skin-side down, for 8–10 minutes until the skin is golden and crispy. Tip in the onion and continue to cook for 5 minutes until the onion softens. Sprinkle in the curry powder and cook for 1 minute more, then stir in the rice and pour over the stock. Bring the stock to the boil.
2 Cover the pan and bake for 30 minutes until all the liquid has been absorbed and the rice is cooked. Stir in the peas and leave the rice to stand for a few minutes before serving.

PER SERVING 445 kcals, protein 32g, carbs 57g, fat 12g, sat fat 3g, fibre 2g, added sugar none, salt 0.5g

One-pan rogan josh

Chicken biryani

Honey mustard chicken pot with parsnips

If you've got time, this casserole will gently bubble away for up to 90 minutes; the meat becomes tender and falls away from the bones.

TAKES 45 MINUTES • SERVES 4

1 tbsp olive oil
8 skinless chicken thighs, bone in
2 onions, finely chopped
350g/12oz parsnips, cut into sticks
300ml/½ pint vegetable stock
2 tbsp wholegrain mustard
2 tbsp clear honey
a few fresh thyme sprigs
flat-leaf parsley, to garnish (optional)
steamed greens, to serve

1 Heat half the oil in a large frying pan or shallow casserole with a lid. Brown the chicken until golden, then set aside. Heat the remaining oil, then cook the onions for 5 minutes until softened.
2 Nestle the thighs back among the onions and add the parsnips. Mix the stock with the mustard and honey, then pour in. Scatter over the thyme, then bring to a simmer. Cover, then cook for 30 minutes (or longer) until the chicken is tender. Season and scatter with parsley, if using, and serve with steamed greens.

PER SERVING 326 kcals, protein 39g, carbs 23g, fat 10g, sat fat 2g, fibre 6g, sugar 15g, salt 0.82g

Roasted ratatouille chicken

A simple method and lovely Mediterranean flavours and colours make this a versatile dish, perfect for either a family supper or a dinner party.

TAKES 50–60 MINUTES • SERVES 4

1 onion, cut into wedges
2 red peppers, deseeded and cut into chunks
1 courgette (about 200g/7oz), cut into chunks
1 small aubergine (about 300g/10oz), cut into chunks
4 tomatoes, halved
4 tbsp olive oil, plus extra for drizzling
4 chicken breasts, skin on (about 140g/5oz each)
a few rosemary sprigs (optional)

1 Heat the oven to 200C/180C fan/gas 6. Lay all the vegetables and the tomatoes in a shallow roasting tin. Make sure they have lots of room – overcrowding will slow down the cooking. Pour over the olive oil and give the vegetables a good mix round until they are well coated (hands are easiest for this).
2 Nestle the chicken breasts on top of the vegetables and tuck in some rosemary sprigs, if you have them. Season everything with salt and black pepper and drizzle a little oil over the chicken. Now roast for about 35 minutes until the vegetables are soft and the chicken is golden. Drizzle with oil before serving.

PER SERVING 318 kcals, protein 37g, carbs 13g, fat 14g, sat fat 2g, fibre 4g, added sugar none, salt 0.25g

Mustard chicken with winter vegetables

This is a great way to make a chicken go further. It takes some time, but is well worth it as you'll get every single bit of flavour from the bird.

TAKES 2 HOURS 40 MINUTES • SERVES 4–6

1 whole chicken, about 1.8kg/4lb
2 onions
6 celery sticks
6 carrots
2 bay leaves
2 fresh thyme sprigs
1 tsp black peppercorns
3 small turnips
50g/2oz butter
100g/3½oz smoked bacon lardons
1 tbsp plain flour
2 tbsp wholegrain mustard
3 rounded tbsp crème fraîche
chopped fresh parsley, to serve

1 Put the chicken in a casserole. Halve an onion, celery stick and carrot. Add to the pot with the herbs, peppercorns and some salt. Add water to halfway up the chicken, boil, then simmer, covered, for 1½ hours. Remove the chicken and strain the stock into a bowl. Chop all remaining veg.
2 Strip the chicken meat from the bones and tear into pieces. Heat the butter in a pan, add the onion and lardons; fry for 5 minutes. Add the remaining veg; fry for 2 minutes. Stir in the flour for 1 minute then add 900ml/1½ pints of the stock, topping up with water if need be. Simmer, covered, for 25 minutes until the vegetables are tender.
3 Add the chicken with the mustard and crème fraîche, simmer, stirring gently. Season and sprinkle with parsley before serving.

PER SERVING 920 kcals, protein 71g, carbs 20g, fat 62g, sat fat 23g, fibre 6g, sugar 14g, salt 3.06g

Pork and apple braise

A low-fat, one-pot dish that's perfect for a family supper. Serve with ready-cooked rice, available from supermarkets.

TAKES 40–45 MINUTES • SERVES 4

500g/1lb 2oz pork tenderloin
1 tbsp plain flour, seasoned
2 tbsp olive oil
1 onion, chopped
1 Cox's apple, cored and cut into thin wedges, skin on
300ml/½ pint chicken or vegetable stock
2 bay leaves
1 tbsp wholegrain mustard
2 tbsp chopped flat-leaf parsley

1 Cut the pork crossways into 2cm/¾ in slices and coat in the seasoned flour. Heat 1 tablespoon of the oil in a large frying pan and fry the pork in small batches, then remove and set aside.
2 Fry the onion in the remaining oil until soft and golden brown. Add the apple and fry until it has slightly caramelised. Slowly stir in the stock, scraping up any bits from the bottom of the pan.
3 Return the pork to the pan and add the bay leaves and mustard. Bring to a simmer and cook for 15–20 minutes, adding a little more water or stock if necessary. Stir in the parsley and season to taste before serving.

PER SERVING 248 kcals, protein 29g, carbs 9g, fat 11g, sat fat 2g, fibre 2g, added sugar none, salt 0.41g

Lamb in palava sauce

Palm oil is an authentic African ingredient that adds a rich red colour – look for oil from Ghana or Sierra Leone in ethnic food shops.

TAKES 1¼–1½ HOURS • SERVES 4

1 red chilli, deseeded and chopped
2.5cm/1in piece fresh root ginger, peeled and
  roughly chopped
2 garlic cloves, peeled
1 onion, half roughly chopped and half sliced
1 tbsp tomato purée
400g can tomatoes
6 tbsp palm or vegetable oil
500g/1lb 2oz lean lamb, cut into 2.5cm/1in
  cubes
300ml/½ pint lamb, chicken or vegetable stock
200g/7oz spinach leaves, roughly shredded
2 eggs, beaten

1 Blitz the chilli, ginger, garlic, chopped onion, tomato purée and tomatoes in a food processor until chopped together to make a sauce.
2 Heat the oil in a large frying pan and fry the sliced onion for 2 minutes. Add the lamb and stir fry over a highish heat for 6–7 minutes until starting to brown. Pour the tomato sauce over the lamb and bubble rapidly for 2–3 minutes, then stir in the stock and add seasoning to taste. Cover and simmer gently for 40–50 minutes, stirring occasionally, until the lamb is tender and the sauce has thickened.
3 Stir the spinach into the sauce so it wilts, then simmer for 2–3 minutes. Drizzle in the egg and continue to simmer for 2 minutes until just set. Serve straight from the pan.

PER SERVING 421 kcals, protein 32g, carbs 3g, fat 31g, sat fat 9g, fibre 1.5g, added sugar none, salt 0.6g

French bean and duck Thai curry

It's really worth making your own Thai curries for their lively freshness of flavour. Duck makes an unusual and luxurious alternative to chicken.

TAKES 2 HOURS • SERVES 4

3–4 duck breasts, about 700g/1lb 9oz total
6 tbsp Thai green curry paste
1 tbsp light brown sugar, plus extra to taste
400ml can coconut milk
2 tbsp fish sauce, plus extra to taste
juice 2 limes
6 kaffir lime leaves, 3 left whole and 3 finely
  shredded
200g/7oz French beans, trimmed
2 handfuls beansprouts
handful of coriander leaves
1 red chilli, deseeded and sliced

1 Place a deep frying pan over a low heat and add the duck breasts, skin-side down. Slowly fry until the golden and there's a pool of fat in the bottom; about 20 minutes. Flip on to the other side for 1 minute, then remove.
2 Pour all but 2 tablespoons of the fat from the pan. Fry the curry paste and sugar for 1–2 minutes then tip in the coconut milk, a can of water, the fish sauce, half the lime juice and the whole lime leaves. Simmer, then slice the duck breasts and add to the curry. Cover, then cook very gently for 1 hour.
3 Add the beans, then simmer, covered, for 10 minutes. Add the remaining lime juice and a little more fish sauce or sugar to season. Stir in the beansprouts, cook for 1 minute more, then serve topped with coriander, the shredded lime leaves and sliced chilli.

PER SERVING 638 kcals, protein 28g, carbs 11g, fat 57g, sat fat 26g, fibre 2g, sugar 9g, salt 2.32g

French bean and duck Thai curry

Lamb in palava sauce

Liver and red pepper stir-fry

Liver is perfect for a mid-week meal as it's so quick to cook. Combine it with a colourful medley of vegetables for a dish bursting with flavour.

TAKES 25–35 MINUTES • SERVES 2

1½ tbsp groundnut oil
200g/7oz lamb's liver, cut into strips
1 leek, diagonally sliced
1 red pepper, deseeded and cut into rough
    squares
1 red chilli, deseeded and finely chopped
1 tsp dried oregano
1 garlic clove, crushed
100g/3½oz spring greens, thinly sliced
grated zest 1 orange and 2 tbsp juice
2 tbsp medium dry sherry

1 Heat 1 tablespoon of the oil in a large non-stick frying pan. Add the liver and stir fry over a moderately high heat for 3 minutes until light brown – don't cook for longer or the liver will become rubbery. Remove to a plate, leaving the juices in the pan.

2 Tip the leek, red pepper and chilli into the pan with the rest of the oil and stir fry over a high heat for 2 minutes. Add the oregano, garlic and greens and stir fry for a further 30 seconds or so, until the greens have just wilted and turned a nice bright green colour.

3 Return the liver to the pan, add the orange zest and juice, and the sherry, then season. Toss everything together on a high heat and serve immediately.

PER SERVING 287 kcals, protein 27g, carbs 11g, fat 14g, sat fat 3g, fibre 4g, added sugar none, salt 0.26g

Broccoli lemon chicken

Tender-stem broccoli is ideal for this dish as it cooks so quickly. Add a couple of minutes to the cooking time if you're using ordinary broccoli.

TAKES 15–25 MINUTES • SERVES 2 GENEROUSLY

1 tbsp groundnut or sunflower oil
340g pack mini chicken breast fillets (sometimes
    called goujons)
2 garlic cloves, sliced
200g pack tender-stem broccoli, stems halved
    if very long
200ml/7fl oz chicken stock
1 heaped tsp cornflour
1 tbsp clear honey or 2 tsp golden caster sugar
grated zest ½ lemon and juice 1 lemon
large handful of roasted cashews

1 Heat the oil in a large frying pan or wok. Add the chicken and fry for 3–4 minutes until golden. Remove from the pan and add the garlic and broccoli. Stir fry for a minute or so, then cover and cook for 2 minutes more, until almost tender.

2 Mix the stock, cornflour and honey or sugar well, then pour into the pan and stir until thickened. Tip the chicken back into the pan and let it heat through, then add the lemon zest and juice and the cashew nuts. Stir, then serve straight away.

PER SERVING 372 kcals, protein 48g, carbs 15g, fat 13g, sat fat 2g, fibre 3g, added sugar 6g, salt 0.69g

Liver and red pepper stir-fry

Broccoli lemon chicken

One-pan duck with Savoy cabbage

Create a smart plated dinner from just one pan with this clever recipe.

TAKES 40 MINUTES • SERVES 4

2 duck breasts, skin on and scored
1 tsp black peppercorns, crushed
600g/1lb 5oz cooked new potatoes, thickly
    sliced
1 bunch flat-leaf parsley, roughly chopped
1 garlic clove, finely chopped
6 rashers smoked streaky bacon, chopped
1 Savoy cabbage, trimmed, quartered, cored
    and finely sliced
1 tbsp balsamic vinegar
2 tbsp olive oil

1 Generously season the duck skin with the peppercorns and a sprinkling of salt. Lay the duck skin-side down in a non-stick sauté pan, then place over a low heat. Leave for 15 minutes to brown and release its fat, then flip over on to the flesh side for 5 minutes.
2 Remove the duck from the pan, then turn up the heat. Add the potatoes to the pan, fry until brown and crisp, then scatter over the parsley and garlic. Scoop out with a slotted spoon on to a plate, then season with salt.
3 Keep the pan on the heat. Fry the bacon until crisp, then add the cabbage. Cook for 1 minute, add a splash of water, then fry for 2 minutes, just until the cabbage is wilted.
4 Meanwhile, mix any duck juices with the vinegar and oil. Slice the duck, serve with the cabbage and potatoes and top with a drizzle of dressing.

PER SERVING 504 kcals, protein 25g, carbs 33g, fat 31g, sat fat 8g, fibre 6g, sugar 7g, salt 1.16g

Rosemary and balsamic chicken with roast onions

A honey glaze adds a lovely sweetness to a classic roast chicken; perfect against the tangy sweetness of roasted red onions.

TAKES ABOUT 2 HOURS • SERVES 4

1 whole chicken, about 1.5kg/3lb 5oz
1 bunch fresh rosemary
4 red onions, peeled and trimmed but left whole
3 tbsp olive oil
3 tbsp balsamic vinegar
1 tbsp clear honey

1 Heat the oven to 190C/170C fan/gas 5. Starting at the neck, carefully loosen the breast skin away from the flesh. Place a sprig of rosemary down each side; put the rest in the cavity. Season the chicken, place in a roasting tin, then sit an onion in each corner of the tin. Drizzle the olive oil over everything then roast for 1 hour 20 minutes.
2 Meanwhile, stir the vinegar and honey together. After 40 minutes, take the chicken from the oven, drizzle the vinegar mix over the chicken and onions, then continue to roast.
3 At the end of the cooking time, remove the chicken from the tin, cover loosely with foil and set aside to rest for 20 minutes. Meanwhile, turn the onions over and continue to roast them until soft. Serve everything up with some of the sticky pan juices.

PER SERVING 629 kcals, protein 48g, carbs 15g, fat 42g, sat fat 11g, fibre 2g, sugar 12g, salt 0.44g

One-pan duck with Savoy cabbage

Rosemary and balsamic chicken with roast onions

Corned beef hash

This is a basic, economical but still completely delicious one-pan supper. Serve with plenty of ketchup, Worcestershire or brown sauce.

TAKES 50 MINUTES • SERVES 4

4 tbsp vegetable oil
900g–1kg/2–2¼lb large potatoes, cut into
    small chunks
knob of butter
1 large onion, roughly chopped
340g can corned beef, cut into chunks

1 Heat 2 tablespoons oil in a large non-stick frying pan, then fry the potatoes for 5 minutes, stirring often. Add a cup of water to the pan and let it boil and bubble off for 5 minutes more until the potatoes are just tender. Tip out on to a plate.
2 Put the butter and 1 tablespoon more oil into the pan over a high heat. Once foaming, tip in the onion and cook for 5 minutes until golden. Pour in the remaining oil, turn up the heat then tip in the potatoes and corned beef. Season.
3 Cook for 15 minutes, folding and turning the hash every 2–3 minutes until you get lots of golden crispy bits. Reduce the heat halfway to medium–low; cook for 5 minutes more, folding and turning the hash every so often. Season, then serve from the pan.

PER SERVING 487 kcals, protein 28g, carbs 42g, fat 24g, sat fat 7g, fibre 4g, added sugar none, salt 2.14g

Bangers and beans in a pan

Perfect for a quick after-work meal. And it's so easy to double or treble the quantities to feed a crowd.

TAKES 35–45 MINUTES • SERVES 4

1 tbsp vegetable oil
454g pack good-quality sausages, each sausage
    chopped into three
1 small onion, chopped
3 carrots, chopped into thick slices
4 celery sticks, sliced into chunks (finely chop
    the leaves if there are any)
2 x 410g cans mixed pulses (or other beans),
    drained and rinsed
400ml/14fl oz chicken or vegetable stock
1–2 tbsp Dijon mustard (or 2 tsp ready-made
    English mustard)
small handful of parsley, chopped
crusty bread, to serve

1 Heat the oil over a highish heat in a wide shallow pan that has a lid. Put the chopped sausages into the pan and sizzle for 5 minutes, stirring occasionally, until they are browned on all sides.
2 Throw in the onion, carrots and celery (not the leaves) and cook for 5 minutes until the onion looks see-through. Tip in the beans, give a good stir, then pour in the stock and bring to the boil, stirring. Cover and simmer for 10–15 minutes until the carrots are tender.
3 Stir in the mustard and parsley with any chopped celery leaves, then season to taste with salt and pepper. Serve hot, with chunks of crusty bread to mop up the sauce.

PER SERVING 479 kcals, protein 26g, carbs 38g, fat 26g, sat fat 8g, fibre 10g, added sugar none, salt 3.7g

Ham and beans with orange

One of the joys of one-pot cooking is putting dishes into the oven well in advance and then forgetting about them until serving time.

TAKES 2½ HOURS, PLUS OVERNIGHT SOAKING • SERVES 4

250g/9oz dried haricot beans, soaked
   overnight
2 oranges
2 tbsp olive oil
1 large onion, chopped
2 celery sticks, chopped
450g/1lb piece gammon, cut into large chunks
1 tbsp paprika
3 tbsp dark muscovado sugar
1 tbsp black treacle or molasses
2 tbsp white wine vinegar
2–3 tbsp tomato purée
4 whole cloves

1 Drain and rinse the beans, then tip them into a pan and pour in 1.4 litres/2½ pints boiling water. Bring to the boil, cover and simmer for 30 minutes.
2 Meanwhile, heat the oven to 180C/160C fan/gas 4. Grate the zest from the oranges; set aside. Heat the oil in a large flameproof casserole. Add the onion and celery and fry, stirring occasionally, for 8 minutes, until the onion is golden. Add the gammon and paprika and stir for 1 minute, then tip in the orange zest, sugar, treacle, vinegar, tomato purée and cloves. Stir well.
3 Tip the beans and cooking liquid into the casserole, cover and cook for 1 hour. Remove the lid and cook for a further hour. Peel the oranges and cut the flesh into chunks. Stir into the beans, with plenty of seasoning.

PER SERVING 493 kcals, protein 37g, carbs 63g, fat 12g, sat fat 3g, fibre 13g, added sugar 19g, salt 2.85g

Sunday brunch beans

Baked beans are great, cheap comfort food, and they're nutritious, too.

TAKES 20–25 MINUTES • SERVES 2 (EASILY DOUBLED)

2 tbsp vegetable oil
1 potato, thinly sliced (unpeeled)
200g can corned beef, sliced
400g can baked beans
splash of Worcestershire sauce

1 Heat the oil in a frying pan until hot, add the potato slices and fry for 7–10 minutes or until golden and crisp.
2 Push the potatoes to one side, add the corned beef and fry undisturbed for a couple of minutes. Tip in the baked beans, add a splash of Worcestershire sauce and stir gently until the beans are hot.

PER SERVING 510 kcals, protein 37g, carbs 40g, fat 23g, sat fat 6.4g, fibre 8.1g, added sugar 6.9g, salt 4.93g

Braised pork with fennel

You can ensure your family stays healthy with this low-fat feast.

TAKES 1¼–1½ HOURS • SERVES 4

1 tbsp olive oil
500g/1lb 2oz pork tenderloin, cut into chunks
1 large onion, chopped
3 garlic cloves, crushed
2 x 400g cans chopped tomatoes
2 tbsp tomato purée
½ tsp caster sugar
200ml/7fl oz vegetable stock
1 large bulb fennel
grated zest 1 lemon

1 Heat 1 teaspoon of the oil in a large pan. Brown the pork on all sides (you may need to do this in batches). Remove from the pan with a slotted spoon and set aside. Add the remaining oil and the onion and cook over a low heat, stirring occasionally, for 5–6 minutes until the onion is soft. Stir in the garlic, tomatoes, tomato purée, sugar, stock and pork, then season. Bring to the boil.

2 Trim the fronds from the fennel, roughly chop and set aside. Cut the bulb into thin wedges and stir into the pork. Push the fennel under the surface of the sauce, lower the heat and simmer for 35–40 minutes with the lid on, until tender. Stir in the lemon zest, garnish with the chopped fennel fronds and serve.

PER SERVING 242 kcals, protein 31g, carbs 12g, fat 8g, sat fat 2g, fibre 4g, added sugar 1g, salt 0.83g

Lincolnshire sausage and lentil simmer

You can offer this one-pot to just about anyone – kids and adults alike. The Puy lentils and pancetta make it a bit special, and everyone loves sausages.

TAKES 1½ HOURS • SERVES 6

1 tbsp vegetable oil
130g pack cubed pancetta or diced bacon
2 packs Lincolnshire pork or other good-quality
   sausages
2 onions, roughly chopped
1 large carrot, chopped
4 garlic cloves, roughly chopped
3 fresh rosemary sprigs
300g/10oz Puy lentils
900ml/1½ pints hot chicken stock
1 tbsp white wine vinegar
400g can chopped tomatoes
2 tbsp chopped flat-leaf parsley, to garnish

1 Heat the oil in a large casserole or very large sauté pan with a lid. Add the pancetta or bacon and the sausages, and sizzle for 10 minutes, turning the sausages occasionally until nicely browned and sticky. Scoop the sausages out on to a plate.

2 Add the onions, carrot and garlic to the pancetta and continue to cook for 3–4 minutes until the onions soften. Return the sausages to the pan and add the rosemary, lentils, stock, vinegar and tomatoes, then season with salt and pepper. Bring to the boil and simmer rapidly for 5 minutes, then lower the heat, cover and simmer for 45 minutes, stirring every so often until the lentils are tender. Check the seasoning, scatter over the parsley and serve from the pan.

PER SERVING 640 kcals, protein 39g, carbs 37g, fat 37g, sat fat 13g, fibre 6g, added sugar none, salt 4.24g

Braised pork with fennel

Lincolnshire sausage and lentil simmer

Greek lamb with orzo

All this needs is some crusty bread and perhaps a salad, and you're looking at a real feast. Orzo looks like large grains of rice, but is actually pasta. If you can't find it, use another small pasta, like trofie.

TAKES ABOUT 3 HOURS • SERVES 6

1kg/2lb 4oz boned shoulder of lamb
2 onions, sliced
1 tbsp chopped fresh oregano, or 1 tsp dried
2 cinnamon sticks, broken in half
½ tsp ground cinnamon
2 tbsp olive oil
400g can chopped tomatoes
1.2 litres/2 pints hot vegetable or chicken stock
400g/14oz orzo
freshly grated Parmesan, to garnish

1 Heat the oven to 180C/160C fan/gas 4. Cut the lamb into 4cm chunks, then spread over the base of a large, wide casserole dish. Add the onions, oregano, cinnamon sticks, ground cinnamon and olive oil, then stir well. Bake, uncovered, for around 45 minutes, stirring halfway.
2 Pour over the chopped tomatoes and stock, cover tightly, then return to the oven for 1½ hours, until the lamb is very tender.
3 Remove the cinnamon sticks, then stir in the orzo. Cover again, then cook for a further 20 minutes, stirring halfway through. The orzo should be cooked and the sauce thickened. Sprinkle with grated Parmesan and serve.

PER SERVING 696 kcals, protein 40g, carbs 58g, fat 36g, sat fat 16g, fibre 4g, sugar 7g, salt 0.68g

Spicy beef stew with beans and peppers

A warming winter twist on chilli con carne; perfect for Bonfire Night. It's made with chunks of braising steak instead of mince for a meltingly tender result.

TAKES 3 HOURS • SERVES 6–8

3½ tbsp vegetable oil
1kg/2lb 4oz stewing beef, cut into chunks
1 onion, sliced
2 garlic cloves, sliced
1 tbsp plain flour
1 tbsp black treacle
1 tsp ground cumin
400g can chopped tomatoes
600ml/1 pint beef stock
2 red peppers, deseeded and sliced
400g can cannellini beans, drained and rinsed
soured cream and fresh coriander, to garnish
crusty bread, to serve

1 Heat 1 tablespoon oil in a large pan with a lid. Season the meat, then cook about one-third of it over a high heat for 10 minutes until browned. Tip on to a plate and repeat with 2 tablespoons oil and rest of the meat.
2 Add a splash of water and scrape the bottom of the pan. Add ½ tablespoon oil. Turn down the heat; fry the onion and garlic until softened. Return the meat to the pan, add the flour and stir for 1 minute. Add the treacle, cumin, tomatoes and stock. Bring to the boil, reduce the heat, cover, then simmer for 1¾ hours. Stir occasionally and check that the meat is covered with liquid.
3 Add the peppers and beans, and cook for a further 15 minutes. Serve in bowls, with a dollop of soured cream and sprinkling of coriander, and bread to serve.

PER SERVING 400 kcals, protein 43g, carbs 18g, fat 18g, sat fat 5g, fibre 4g, sugar 8g, salt 1.2g

Spicy beef stew with beans and peppers

Greek lamb with orzo

Quick meatball casserole

Low-fat, delicious and healthy – and all in one pot, too!

TAKES 45–50 MINUTES • SERVES 4

500g/1lb 2oz turkey mince
small bunch of parsley, chopped
1 tbsp olive oil
2 large onions, chopped
2 garlic cloves, crushed
450g/1lb carrots, quartered, then cut into
    chunks
450g/1lb potatoes, peeled and cut into chunks
1 tbsp paprika
500g jar passata (sieved tomatoes)

1 Mix the turkey mince with half the chopped parsley, and salt and pepper to taste, then shape into 12 balls. Heat the oil in a large non-stick pan or flameproof casserole and fry the meatballs for 4–5 minutes, shaking the pan occasionally, until the meat is browned all over.
2 Add the chopped onions, garlic, carrots, potatoes and 300ml/½ pint water to the pan. Bring to the boil, cover and simmer for 15 minutes.
3 Stir in the paprika, passata and half the remaining parsley. Bring to the boil, cover and cook for a further 10–15 minutes or until the potatoes and carrots are tender. Season to taste and sprinkle with the remaining parsley to serve.

PER SERVING 330 kcals, protein 32g, carbs 38g, fat 6g, sat fat 1.5g, fibre 6g, added sugar none, salt 0.38g

Hearty lamb and barley soup

Come home to a bowl of this hearty soup on a cold winter's day. Pearl barley plumps up as it cooks and thickens the soup beautifully.

TAKES 35 MINUTES • SERVES 4

1 tsp olive oil
200g/7oz lamb neck fillet, trimmed of fat and cut
    into small pieces
½ large onion, finely chopped
50g/2oz pearl barley
600g/1lb 5oz mixed root vegetables (we used
    potato, parsnip and swede, peeled and
    cubed)
2 tsp Worcestershire sauce
1 litre/1¾ pints lamb or beef stock
1 fresh thyme sprig
100g/3½oz green beans (frozen are fine), halved
granary bread, to serve

1 Heat the oil in a large pan. Season the lamb, then fry for a few minutes until browned. Add the onion and barley, then gently fry for 1 minute. Add the veg, cook for 2 more minutes, then add the Worcestershire sauce, stock and thyme. Cover, then simmer for 20 minutes.
2 When everything is cooked, spoon about a quarter of the soup into a blender or processor and whizz, then stir it back into the rest of the soup. Add the green beans, simmer for 3 minutes, then ladle the soup into bowls and serve with granary bread.

PER SERVING 258 kcals, protein 17g, carbs 26g, fat 11g, sat fat 4g, fibre 4g, sugar 12g, salt 1.48g

Quick meatball casserole

Hearty lamb and barley soup

Coddled pork with cider

You could use lamb chops for this recipe, if you prefer. Simply trim the excess fat off the chops before browning.

TAKES 35 MINUTES • SERVES 2 (EASILY DOUBLED)

small knob of butter
2 pork loin chops
4 rashers smoked bacon, cut into pieces
1 carrot, cut into large chunks
2 potatoes, cut into chunks
½ small swede, cut into chunks
¼ large cabbage, cut into smaller wedges
1 bay leaf
100ml/3½fl oz cider
100ml/3½fl oz chicken stock

1 Heat the butter in a casserole dish until sizzling, then fry the pork for 2–3 minutes on each side until browned. Remove from the pan. Tip the bacon, carrot, potatoes and swede into the pan, then gently fry until slightly coloured.
2 Stir in the cabbage, sit the chops back on top, add the bay leaf, then pour over the cider and stock. Cover the pan, then leave everything to simmer gently for 20 minutes until the pork is cooked through and the vegetables are tender. Serve at the table spooned straight from the dish.

PER SERVING 717 kcals, protein 44g, carbs 37g, fat 44g, sat fat 17g, fibre 12g, sugar 20g, salt 2.59g

Rosemary roast chops and potatoes

A quick one-pan family roast that won't leave you arguing about the washing up!

TAKES 40 MINUTES • SERVES 4

3 tbsp olive oil
8 lamb chops
1kg/2lb 4oz potatoes, chopped into small chunks
4 fresh rosemary sprigs
4 garlic cloves, left whole
250g/9oz cherry tomatoes
1 tbsp balsamic vinegar

1 Heat the oven to 220C/200C fan/gas 7. Heat half the oil in a flameproof roasting tin or a shallow ovenproof casserole. Brown the lamb for 2 minutes on each side, then lift out of the pan. Add the rest of the oil, throw in the potatoes and fry for 4–5 minutes until starting to brown. Toss in the rosemary and garlic, then nestle the lamb in along with the potatoes.
2 Roast everything together for 20 minutes, then scatter over the tomatoes and drizzle with the vinegar. Place back in the oven for 5 minutes until the tomatoes just begin to split. Remove from the oven and serve straight from the dish.

PER SERVING 754 kcals, protein 36g, carbs 46g, fat 48g, sat fat 21g, fibre 4g, sugar 4g, salt 0.34g

Steak and sticky red-wine shallots

To turn this recipe into a quick coq au vin, make it with chicken breasts, leaving them in the pan as the wine reduces.

TAKES 25 MINUTES • SERVES 2

8 shallots, peeled and quartered
2 sirloin steaks, about 175g/6oz each
crushed black peppercorns, to taste
25g/1oz butter
4 tbsp balsamic vinegar
1 large glass red wine, about 175ml/6fl oz
150ml/¼ pint beef stock

1 Half-fill a frying pan with water. Boil; simmer the shallots for 2–3 minutes, then drain and set aside.
2 Season the steaks with a little salt and plenty of crushed peppercorns. Heat half the butter in the pan until sizzling, then cook the steaks for 3 minutes on each side for medium or until done to your liking.
3 Remove the steaks and keep warm. While they rest, add the remaining butter to the pan, throw in the shallots, then sizzle in the sticky pan until starting to brown. Add the balsamic vinegar and bubble for a few minutes. Add the wine and boil down until sticky, then add the beef stock and simmer until everything comes together. Spoon the shallots over the steaks and serve.

PER SERVING 524 kcals, protein 40g, carbs 10g, fat 33g, sat fat 16g, fibre 1g, sugar 10g, salt 1.87g

Quick and creamy steak with onion

This great little treat is easy to rustle up when you fancy something a bit special that won't take an age to put together.

TAKES 30 MINUTES • SERVES 2 (EASILY DOUBLED)

300g/10oz rump steak
1 tsp seasoned plain flour
generous knob of butter
drizzle of olive oil
1 red onion, finely chopped
175g/6oz chestnut mushrooms, sliced
2 tsp wholegrain mustard
142ml pot soured cream

1 Thinly slice the steak into long strips across the grain, trimming off any fat. Toss the strips in a teaspoon of seasoned flour.
2 Heat the butter and olive oil in a frying pan, then add the onion and fry for about 8 minutes, until softened and lightly coloured. Add the meat and quickly stir-fry until browned all over. Add the mushrooms and cook for 3 minutes, or until softened.
3 Season well with salt and freshly ground black pepper, then stir in the mustard and soured cream and bring to a gentle simmer, stirring, to make a smooth, creamy sauce.

PER SERVING 502 kcals, protein 38g, carbs 9g, fat 35g, sat fat 17g, fibre 2g, sugar 6g, salt 0.93g

Pork ragout with carrots and cumin

A superhealthy stew for all the family. The kids will enjoy the sweet flavours from the carrots and raisins, and everyone will love the mild spices.

TAKES 55 MINUTES • SERVES 4

1 tbsp olive oil
450g/1lb pork fillet, trimmed of all visible fat
   and cut into cubes
2 large onions, sliced
450g/1lb carrots, sliced thickly and diagonally
2 tsp ground cumin
½ tsp ground cinnamon
2 tbsp tomato purée
100g/3½oz raisins
1 tbsp each toasted sesame seeds and
   chopped fresh coriander, to garnish
bread or rice, to serve

1 Heat the oil in a large pan, add the pork, then fry until the meat is sealed. Lift on to a plate. Add the onions, fry until lightly coloured, then stir in the carrots, spices, tomato purée and raisins. Add 450ml/16fl oz water, then bring to the boil.
2 Cover, gently cook for 25 minutes until the carrots are tender, add the pork to the pan, then simmer for 5 minutes until cooked through. Scatter over the sesame seeds and coriander, then serve with bread or rice.

PER SERVING 328 kcals, protein 28g, carbs 34g, fat 10g, sat fat 2g, fibre 5g, sugar 30g, salt 0.35g

Oven-baked risotto

Cook this simple storecupboard risotto in the oven while you get on with something else – the result is still wonderfully creamy.

TAKES 30–35 MINUTES • SERVES 4

250g pack smoked bacon, chopped into
   small pieces
1 onion, chopped
25g/1oz butter
300g/10oz risotto rice
half a glass of white wine (optional)
150g pack cherry tomatoes, halved
700ml/1¼ pint chicken stock (from a cube
   is fine)
50g/2oz Parmesan, grated

1 Heat the oven to 200C/180C fan/gas 6. Fry the bacon pieces in an ovenproof pan or casserole dish for 3–5 minutes until golden and crisp. Stir in the onion and butter and cook for 3–4 minutes until soft. Tip in the rice and mix well until coated. Pour over the wine, if using, and cook for 2 minutes until absorbed.
2 Add the cherry tomatoes and the hot stock, then give the rice a quick stir. Cover with a tightly fitting lid and bake for 18 minutes until just cooked.
3 Stir through most of the Parmesan and serve sprinkled with the remainder.

PER SERVING 517 kcals, protein 22g, carbs 63g, fat 20g, sat fat 10g, fibre 2g, added sugar none, salt 3.38g

Oven-baked risotto

Pork ragout with carrots and cumin

Irish stew

The trick with this classic one-pot is to use a cheap cut of meat, which means you'll skimp on price but not quality. Middle neck (neck fillets) or scrag end are both really flavoursome and perfect for braising.

TAKES 2½ HOURS • SERVES 6

1 tbsp sunflower oil
200g/7oz smoked streaky bacon, preferably in one piece, skinned and cut into chunks
900g/2lb stewing lamb, cut into large chunks
5 medium onions, sliced
5 carrots, cut into chunks
3 bay leaves
1 small bunch fresh thyme
100g/3½oz pearl barley
900ml/1½ pints lamb stock
6 medium potatoes, cut into chunks
small knob of butter
3 spring onions, finely sliced, to garnish

1 Heat the oven to 160C/140C fan/gas 3. Heat the oil in a flameproof casserole. Sizzle the bacon for 4 minutes until crisp. Turn up the heat, add the lamb and brown for 6 minutes. Remove with a slotted spoon. Add the onions, carrots and herbs to the pan, then soften for 5 minutes. Return the meat to the pan, stir in the pearl barley and stock, then bring to a simmer.
2 Sit the chunks of potato on top of the stew, cover, then braise in the oven, undisturbed, for about 1½ hours until the potatoes are soft and the meat is tender. Remove from the oven, dot the potatoes with butter, scatter with the spring onions and serve scooped straight from the dish.

PER SERVING 627 kcals, protein 49g, carbs 44g, fat 30g, sat fat 14g, fibre 5g, sugar 11g, salt 2.13g

Classic Swedish meatballs

All these need is some crusty bread – though they're especially delicious with a spoonful of cranberry jelly or sauce.

TAKES 35 MINUTES • SERVES 4

400g/14oz lean minced pork
1 egg, beaten
1 small onion, finely chopped or grated
85g/3oz fresh white breadcrumbs
1 tbsp finely chopped fresh dill, plus extra to garnish
1 tbsp each olive oil and butter
2 tbsp plain flour
400ml/14fl oz hot beef stock

1 In a bowl, mix the mince with the egg, onion, breadcrumbs, dill and some seasoning. Form into small meatballs about the size of walnuts – you should get about 20.
2 Heat the olive oil in a large non-stick frying pan and brown the meatballs. You may have to do this in two batches. Remove from the pan, melt the butter, then sprinkle over the flour and stir well. Cook for 2 minutes, then slowly whisk in the stock. Keep whisking until it is a thick gravy, then return the meatballs to the pan and heat through. Sprinkle with dill and serve.

PER SERVING 301 kcals, protein 26g, carbs 22g, fat 13g, sat fat 4g, fibre 1g, sugar 2g, salt 1.73g

Irish stew

Classic Swedish meatballs

Sausage and leek hash

You can use any leftover vegetables for this simple weekend supper.

TAKES 30–35 MINUTES • SERVES 4

2 tbsp olive oil
6 plump sausages
6 potatoes, thinly sliced
350g/12oz thinly sliced leeks (or broccoli or
    cabbage)
1 tbsp creamed horseradish sauce, or more
    to taste
100g/3½oz mature Cheddar or Gruyère, grated

1 Heat half of the oil in a large heavy-based frying pan. Add the sausages and fry gently for 8–10 minutes until well browned. Remove the sausages, then slice them on the diagonal and set aside.
2 Turn the heat to medium and add the remaining oil. Add the potatoes and leeks and give everything a good stir. Cook until the potatoes and leeks are tender and beginning to brown, turning them over from time to time. This will take 15–20 minutes.
3 Toss the sausages back in along with the horseradish, to taste, and heat through for a further 2–3 minutes. Take the pan off the heat, sprinkle in the cheese, season well and stir gently to combine. Serve.

PER SERVING 534 kcals, protein 24g, carbs 35g, fat 34g, sat fat 13.5g, fibre 4g, added sugar 0.3g, salt 2.46g

Frying-pan sausage hotpot

Ready-sliced, cooked, long-life potatoes make this a really speedy supper dish.

TAKES 25–35 MINUTES • SERVES 3

1 tbsp vegetable oil
6 plump good-quality sausages with herbs
splash of red wine (if you have some)
175ml/6fl oz vegetable stock
3 tbsp ready-prepared caramelised red onions
400g pack cooked sliced long-life potatoes

1 Heat the oil in a medium frying pan (one into which the sausages will fit fairly snugly). Add the sausages and fry for 8–10 minutes, turning them often. Heat the grill to high. Splash a couple of tablespoons of red wine, if you are using it, into the pan, then pour in the stock and stir in the caramelised red onions. Allow the mixture to bubble for 3–4 minutes, so it thickens a little and turns into a rich gravy. Remove from the heat.
2 Spread the potatoes so they roughly cover the sausages and gravy. Put the frying pan under the grill for about 8 minutes until the potatoes turn crisp and golden. Serve while bubbling and hot – there is no need to add seasoning.

PER SERVING 578 kcals, protein 20g, carbs 36g, fat 40g, sat fat 14g, fibre 4g, added sugar 1g, salt 5.07g

Cheesy chops and chips

Get your protein hit with this all-in-one roast.

TAKES 1–1¼ HOURS • SERVES 4

1kg/2lb 4oz potatoes, peeled and thickly sliced
1 onion, thinly sliced
splash of cider, wine, water or stock
2 tbsp olive oil
4 pork chops, about 175g/6oz each
100g/3½oz Cheddar, grated
1 tbsp wholegrain mustard
3 tbsp milk

1 Heat the oven to 230C/210C fan/gas 8. Toss the potatoes, onion, liquid and oil together in a large flameproof casserole. Season if you like, then bake for 20–30 minutes until the potatoes start to brown. Lay the chops on the potatoes and cook for 10 minutes more.
2 Mix the cheese, mustard and milk together. When the chops have had 10 minutes in the oven, spread the cheese mixture over them and switch the oven over to grill. Place the pan under the grill and cook for about 5 minutes until the cheese is bubbling and the potatoes are golden and crispy. Serve straight from the pan.

PER SERVING 580 kcals, protein 42g, carbs 40g, fat 32g, sat fat 14g, fibre 5g, added sugar none, salt 1.6g

Pizza chicken melts

With only five ingredients this is a great after-work meal.

TAKES 10–15 MINUTES • SERVES 2 (EASILY HALVED OR DOUBLED)

2 small boneless, skinless chicken breasts
1 tbsp olive oil
50g/2oz Cheddar, grated
4 cherry tomatoes, quartered
2 tsp pesto
green salad, to serve

1 Heat the grill to high. Sandwich the chicken between cling film or 2 plastic food bags and beat firmly with a rolling pin or the bottom of a saucepan to flatten. Heat the oil in a non-stick frying pan, add the chicken and cook for 2 minutes on each side until golden.
2 While the chicken cooks, mix the cheese and tomatoes together. Take the chicken from the pan and wipe out the oil with kitchen paper. Return the chicken to the pan, spread each breast with a teaspoon of pesto, then pile the cheese and tomatoes on top.
3 Put under the hot grill for a minute or so (protect the handle with foil if you think it is likely to burn), until the cheese has melted. Serve with a green salad.

PER SERVING 315 kcals, protein 37g, carbs 1g, fat 18g, sat fat 8g, fibre none, added sugar none, salt 0.68g

Prawn pilau, page 117

Fish and seafood

20-minute seafood pasta

For a Spanish-style version, add a pinch of saffron and a little white wine along with the tomatoes.

TAKES 20–25 MINUTES • SERVES 4

1 tbsp olive oil
1 onion, chopped
1 garlic clove, chopped
1 tsp paprika
400g can chopped tomatoes
1 litre/1¾ pints chicken stock
300g/10oz spaghetti, roughly broken
240g pack mixed frozen seafood, defrosted
TO SERVE
handful of parsley leaves, chopped
4 lemon wedges

1 Heat the oil in a wok or large frying pan, then cook the onion and garlic over a medium heat for 5 minutes until soft. Add the paprika, tomatoes and stock, then bring to the boil.
2 Turn down the heat to a simmer, stir in the pasta and cook for 7 minutes, stirring occasionally to stop the pasta from sticking.
3 Stir in the seafood, cook for 3 minutes more until it's all heated through and the pasta is cooked, then season to taste. Sprinkle with the parsley and serve with lemon wedges.

PER SERVING 370 kcals, protein 23g, carbs 62g, fat 5g, sat fat 1g, fibre 4g, added sugar none, salt 1.4g

Haddock in tomato basil sauce

One-pot dishes are often healthy as well as simple. This easy fish recipe proves that reducing fat doesn't mean reducing flavour.

TAKES 40–50 MINUTES • SERVES 4

1 tbsp olive oil
1 onion, thinly sliced
1 small aubergine, about 250g/9oz, roughly chopped
½ tsp paprika
2 garlic cloves, crushed
400g can chopped tomatoes
1 tsp dark or light muscovado sugar
8 large basil leaves, plus a few extra for sprinkling
4 x 175g/6oz firm skinless white fish fillets, such as haddock
salad and crusty bread, to serve

1 Heat the oil in a large non-stick frying pan and stir fry the onion and aubergine for about 4 minutes until they start to turn golden. Cover with a lid and let the vegetables steam fry in their own juices for 6 minutes – this helps them to soften without needing any extra oil.
2 Stir in the paprika, garlic, tomatoes and sugar with ½ teaspoon salt and cook for 8–10 minutes, stirring often, until the vegetables are tender.
3 Scatter in the basil leaves, then nestle the fish in the sauce. Cover and cook for 6–8 minutes until the fish flakes easily when tested with a fork. Tear over the rest of the basil and serve with a salad and crusty bread.

PER SERVING 212 kcals, protein 36g, carbs 8g, fat 4g, sat fat 1g, fibre 3g, added sugar 1g, salt 0.5g

20-minute seafood pasta

Haddock in tomato basil sauce

Fish with lemon and beans

This is a speedy supper dish that gives you a great sense of well being. Try stirring in capers, olives or peppers for a slightly different taste.

TAKES 10–15 MINUTES • SERVES 2

400g can butter beans, drained and rinsed
3 tbsp lemon-infused olive oil or 3 tbsp olive oil
    mixed with a little lemon juice
2 handfuls parsley leaves, roughly chopped
100g/3½oz piece chorizo sausage, skinned and
    chopped into small chunks
2 x 175g/6oz skinless white fish fillets,
    such as cod

1 Tip the butter beans into a shallow microwave dish. Stir in half the lemon oil, half the parsley and all the chorizo. Top with the fish fillets and the remaining oil. Cover the dish with cling film and pierce a few times. Microwave on High for 4–5 minutes, until the fish looks opaque and flakes easily.
2 Remove the fish from the dish. Stir the beans and chorizo together and spoon on to plates. Top with the fish and scatter with the remaining parsley.

PER SERVING 523 kcals, protein 48g, carbs 17g, fat 30g, sat fat 7g, fibre 6g, added sugar none, salt 2g

Tomato and thyme cod

So few ingredients, yet this dish really performs. The soy sauce adds a deep, savoury flavour to the tomatoes.

TAKES 20 MINUTES • SERVES 4

1 tbsp olive oil
1 onion, chopped
400g can chopped tomatoes
1 heaped tsp light brown soft sugar
a few fresh thyme sprigs, leaves stripped
1 tbsp soy sauce
4 sustainably caught white fish fillets

1 Heat the oil in a frying pan, add the onion, then fry for 5–8 minutes until lightly browned. Stir in the tomatoes, sugar, thyme and soy sauce, then bring to the boil. Simmer for 5 minutes, then slip the fish into the sauce.
2 Cover and gently cook for 8–10 minutes until the cod flakes easily.

PER SERVING 172 kcals, protein 27g, carbs 7g, fat 4g, sat fat 1g, fibre 1g, sugar 6g, salt 1.1g

Fish with lemon and beans

Tomato and thyme cod

Caribbean fish stew

Angostura bitters is a concentrated flavouring for food and drink, made from a secret blend of herbs and spices.

TAKES 30–40 MINUTES, PLUS OPTIONAL MARINATING • SERVES 2

grated zest and juice 1 lime
2 x 175–200g/6–7oz skinless white fish fillets, such as cod, haddock, hoki or pollock
juice 2 lemons
2 x 15g packs fresh thyme, leaves stripped from the stalks
1 tbsp dark rum
3 tbsp vegetable oil
1 onion, cut into rings
handful of fresh coriander, chopped
2 garlic cloves, chopped
1 beefsteak tomato or 3 regular ones, sliced
2 tsp dark muscovado sugar
dash of Angostura bitters (optional)
2 lime halves, to serve

1 Spread the lime zest and juice over the base of a shallow glass or ceramic dish. Lay the fish in the dish and pour over the lemon juice. Using a mortar and pestle, crush the thyme leaves to a rough paste with ¼ teaspoon white pepper and a pinch of salt. Rub the paste all over the fish, then sprinkle over the rum. Cover and marinate at room temperature for 1 hour, if you have time.
2 Heat the oil in a deep frying pan and fry the onion for 4–5 minutes until softened. Stir in the coriander, garlic, tomato and sugar, and cook for 3–4 minutes.
3 Put the fish and its marinade in the pan, pour over 3 tablespoons water, and the bitters, if you are using them. Cover and cook gently for 6–8 minutes until the fish flakes easily with a fork. Season and serve with the lime halves.

PER SERVING 388 kcals, protein 35g, carbs 17g, fat 19g, sat fat 2g, fibre 2g, added sugar 5g, salt 0.31g

Kerala prawn curry

If you like spicy food, you'll love this curry, with its creamy consistency, crackling curry leaves and coconut flavour.

TAKES 25–35 MINUTES • SERVES 2

2 red chillies, deseeded and quartered lengthways
1 small red onion, chopped
2.5cm/1in fresh root ginger, peeled and chopped
1 tbsp vegetable or sunflower oil
1 tsp black mustard seeds
½ tsp fenugreek seeds
14 curry leaves, fresh or dried
½ tsp turmeric
½ tsp cracked black peppercorns
150ml/¼ pint reduced-fat coconut milk
250g/9oz cooked and peeled jumbo prawns, some with their tails on
TO SERVE
squeeze of lime
chopped fresh coriander, plus a sprig or two

1 In a food processor, blitz the chillies, onion and ginger with 3 tablespoons water to a smoothish paste.
2 Heat the oil in a wide shallow pan or wok. Toss in the mustard and fenugreek seeds and the curry leaves – they crackle and pop – and fry for 10 seconds. Add the onion paste, lower the heat and cook without colouring for about 5 minutes. Splash in some water if it starts to catch.
3 Add the turmeric and peppercorns and stir for a few seconds. Pour in the coconut milk and bring to a simmer, stirring all the time, then lower the heat and add the prawns. Cook for 1–2 minutes until heated through. Squeeze over some lime and sprinkle with coriander before serving.

PER SERVING 294 kcals, protein 31g, carbs 8g, fat 16g, sat fat 8g, fibre none, added sugar none, salt 2.76g

Kerala prawn curry

Caribbean fish stew

Easiest-ever seafood risotto

Risottos make the perfect microwave one-pot dish. Unlike ones cooked on the hob, you don't have to stir, leaving you free to do something else.

TAKES 25–35 MINUTES • SERVES 4

1 onion, finely chopped
1 bulb fennel, finely sliced
1 tbsp olive oil
300g/10oz risotto rice
500ml/18fl oz fish or vegetable stock
300g bag frozen seafood mix, defrosted
100g/3½oz frozen peas
3 tbsp grated Parmesan
grated zest and juice 1 lemon
handful of parsley leaves, roughly chopped

1 Tip the onion and fennel into a large microwave bowl, toss in the oil and microwave on High for 5 minutes. Stir in the rice, pour over the stock and cover the bowl with a plate. Microwave on High for 10–15 minutes more or until the rice is just on the verge of being cooked.
2 Stir in the seafood and peas, cover and continue to microwave on High for 2–3 minutes until the rice is cooked. Stir in the Parmesan and lemon juice, and leave to stand for a couple of minutes while you mix the parsley with the lemon zest. Spoon the risotto into bowls and scatter over the parsley and lemon zest. Serve.

PER SERVING 419 kcals, protein 29g, carbs 64g, fat 7g, sat fat 2g, fibre 4g, added sugar none, salt 1.16g

Sizzling summer cod

You can use salmon instead of cod, if you like, in this fresh and tasty dish.

TAKES 15–20 MINUTES • SERVES 2

250g jar roasted mixed peppers with herbs
250g/9oz new potatoes, scrubbed and thickly sliced
1 red onion, cut into wedges
140g/5oz green beans, trimmed and halved widthways
2 x 175g/6oz chunky cod fillets, skin on
½ lemon
crusty bread, to serve

1 Pour all the oil from the jar of peppers into a deep frying pan. Heat the oil until bubbling, then tip in the potatoes and onion and toss in the oil. Cook for 5 minutes, stirring every now and then, until the potatoes are beginning to turn golden.
2 Carefully pour most of the oil out of the frying pan, leaving behind about 1 tablespoon. Tip in the beans and drained peppers, season and stir until well mixed. Lay the fish, skin-side down, on top of the vegetables.
3 Cover the pan and cook over a medium heat for 5 minutes more or until the fish flakes easily with a fork and the vegetables are tender. Squeeze the lemon half over the fish and serve with crusty bread.

PER SERVING 337 kcals, protein 37g, carbs 32g, fat 8g, sat fat 1g, fibre 5g, added sugar none, salt 0.48g

Easiest-ever seafood risotto

Sizzling summer cod

Speedy salmon and leeks

Serve with crusty bread to mop up the tasty juices.

TAKES 20–25 MINUTES • SERVES 4

700g/1lb 9oz leeks, finely sliced
3 tbsp olive oil
2 tbsp wholegrain mustard
2 tbsp clear honey
juice ½ lemon
250g pack cherry tomatoes, halved
4 x 175g/6oz skinless salmon fillets

1 Put the leeks into a large microwave dish and sprinkle over 2 tablespoons water. Cover the dish with cling film and pierce a couple of times with a fork. Cook on High for 3 minutes, then leave to stand for 1 minute.
2 Whisk the olive oil, mustard, honey and lemon juice together, and season with a little salt and pepper. Scatter the tomatoes on top of the leeks and spoon over half the sauce.
3 Lay the salmon fillets side by side on top of the vegetables and spoon the remaining sauce over them. Replace the cling film and continue cooking on High for 9 minutes. Leave to stand for a couple of minutes before serving.

PER SERVING 471 kcals, protein 39g, carbs 13g, fat 29g, sat fat 6g, fibre 5g, added sugar 6g, salt 0.54g

Savoy cabbage and beans with white fish

This cabbage stew is based on a peasant dish from south-west France and is served with everything from duck to fish.

TAKES 50 MINUTES • SERVES 4

small knob of butter
5 rashers smoked streaky bacon, chopped
1 onion, finely chopped
2 celery sticks, diced
2 carrots, diced
1 small bunch fresh thyme
1 Savoy cabbage, shredded
4 tbsp white wine
300ml/½ pint chicken stock
410g can flageolet beans in water, drained
    and rinsed
FOR THE FISH
2 tbsp olive oil
4 fillets sustainably caught white fish, each
    about 140g/5oz, skin on
2 tbsp plain flour

1 Heat the butter in a large non-stick frying pan until starting to sizzle, add the bacon, then fry for a few minutes. Add the onion, celery and carrots and cook for 8–10 minutes until softening, but not brown. Stir in the thyme and cabbage, then cook for a few minutes until the cabbage starts to wilt.
2 Pour in the wine, simmer until evaporated, then add the stock and beans. Season, cover the pan, then simmer gently for 10 minutes until the cabbage is soft but still vibrant. Spoon the cabbage into serving bowls and keep warm.
3 Wipe out the pan and heat the oil in it. Season each fillet, then dust the skin with flour. Fry the fish, skin-side down, for 4 minutes until crisp, then flip over and finish on the flesh side until cooked through. Serve each fish fillet on top of the cabbage and beans.

PER SERVING 423 kcals, protein 42g, carbs 29g, fat 16g, sat fat 4g, fibre 10g, sugar 13g, salt 1.45g

Parmesan-crusted fish

This is a delicious way of jazzing up white fish.

TAKES 20–30 MINUTES • SERVES 4

50g/2oz fresh breadcrumbs
grated zest and juice 1 lemon
25g/1oz Parmesan, grated
2 tbsp chopped fresh parsley
4 thick firm skinless white fish fillets, such as
    cod, haddock, hoki or pollock
2 tbsp olive oil
50g/2oz butter

1 Heat the grill to high. Mix the breadcrumbs with the lemon zest, Parmesan, parsley, and salt and pepper to taste. Season the fish.
2 Heat the oil in a frying pan. Add the fish, skinned-side down, and fry for 2–3 minutes until the flesh flakes easily with a fork. Turn the fish over and sprinkle with the breadcrumb mixture, then slide the pan under the hot grill and toast the breadcrumb topping for 2–3 minutes. Add the butter to the pan in pieces, pour in the lemon juice and let the butter melt around the fish.
3 Serve the fish with the lemony butter poured over.

PER SERVING 334 kcals, protein 31g, carbs 10g, fat 19g, sat fat 8.6g, fibre 0.4g, added sugar none, salt 0.78g

Smoked haddock with colcannon and mustard

Take the time to cook yourself something special, with this full-flavoured meal for one.

TAKES 30–40 MINUTES • SERVES 1 (EASILY DOUBLED)

200ml/7fl oz vegetable stock
1 medium potato, peeled and chopped into
    small chunks
large handful of kale, spring greens or cabbage,
    finely shredded
small knob of butter
140g/5oz piece smoked skinned haddock
    (undyed is best)
1 heaped tbsp Dijon mustard
25g/1oz melted butter

1 Put the stock and potato in a small pan. Cover and boil for 6 minutes until the potato starts to fluff round the edges and the stock has reduced slightly. Throw in the greens and butter, stir, then cover the pan again, lower the heat and simmer for 4 minutes to soften the kale.
2 Lay the haddock fillet on top of the kale and potatoes, cover the pan and leave to steam gently for 5 minutes. Meanwhile, whisk the mustard, a splash of water and seasoning into the butter. Set aside.
3 Prod a corner of the haddock fillet – it's ready when it flakes easily. Lift out the cooked haddock and put it to one side. Mash the potato and kale together in the pan with the pan juices. Scoop the mash on to a warmed plate, sit the haddock on top and spoon the sauce over.

PER SERVING 459 kcals, protein 34g, carbs 21g, fat 27g, sat fat 15g, fibre 3g, added sugar none, salt 6.21g

Cheesy fish grills

Even those who don't love fish will like this simple, speedy, foolproof dish.

TAKES 15–25 MINUTES • SERVES 4

sunflower or olive oil, for brushing
4 chunky, skinless white fish fillets, such as hoki or cod, about 500g/1lb 2oz total
4 thin, but not wafer-thin, slices ham
50g/2oz mature Cheddar, grated
2 spring onions, sliced at an angle
green salad, to serve

1 Heat the grill to high and lightly oil a large, shallow, flameproof dish. Arrange the fillets, skinned-side down, in the dish, slightly spaced apart, and brush with a little oil. Grill for 2 minutes.
2 Remove the dish from the grill, turn the fish over and top each fillet with a scrunched slice of ham. Mix together the cheese and onions, scatter over the fish and season with salt and pepper. Return to the grill for 5 minutes or until the fish flakes easily with a fork. Serve with a green salad.

PER SERVING 179 kcals, protein 30g, carbs none, fat 6g, sat fat 3g, fibre none, added sugar none, salt 0.94g

Italian-style roasted fish

Let the fresh flavours of the Mediterranean into your home with this delicious one-pot dish.

TAKES 25–30 MINUTES • SERVES 4

4 thick firm white fish fillets, such as cod, haddock, hoki or pollock, skin on
1 tbsp olive oil, plus extra for drizzling
500g/1lb 2oz cherry tomatoes, halved
50g/2oz pitted black olives, halved
25g/1oz pine nuts
large handful of basil leaves

1 Heat the oven to 200C/180C fan/gas 6. Season the fish. Heat the oil in a large roasting tin on top of the stove and cook the fillets, skin-side down, for 2–3 minutes or until just crisp.
2 Scatter the tomatoes, olives and pine nuts around the fish, season and roast in the oven for 12–15 minutes until the fish flakes easily with a fork. Scatter with the basil leaves and drizzle with a little olive oil before serving.

PER SERVING 242 kcals, protein 30g, carbs 4g, fat 12g, sat fat 1.5g, fibre 1.7g, added sugar none, salt 0.99g

Cheesy fish grills

Italian-style roasted fish

Zesty roast salmon and cod

Roasting is a foolproof way of cooking fish. In this recipe the fish stays moist and the peppers become soft and sweet.

TAKES ABOUT 1 HOUR (OR LONGER, DEPENDING ON MARINATING) • SERVES 8

800g/1lb 12oz thick skinless salmon fillet, cut into 8
800g/1lb 12oz thick skinless sustainably caught cod loin, cut into 8
85g/3oz raisins
3 tbsp olive oil
zest and juice 2 oranges
3 red peppers, halved, deseeded and cut into 6
3 orange peppers, halved, deseeded and cut into 6
50g/2oz toasted pine nuts
large handful of flat-leaf parsley, roughly chopped, to garnish

1 Place the fish and raisins in a large bowl, add 2 tablespoons olive oil and the orange zest and juice, and season well. Carefully toss the fish to coat, cover, and leave to marinate for 30 minutes or up to 2 hours. Heat the oven to 200C/180C fan/gas 6.
2 Meanwhile, place the peppers in a large, shallow roasting tin and drizzle with the remaining olive oil. Season, toss together and roast in the oven for 30 minutes.
3 Arrange the fish and raisins on top of the peppers and pour over the juices. Scatter the pine nuts over and season with a good pinch of salt. Cook in the oven for 12–15 minutes until the fish is just cooked through. Scatter with parsley and bring to the table.

PER SERVING 407 kcals, protein 41g, carbs 15g, fat 21g, sat fat 3g, fibre 2g, added sugar none, salt 0.3g

Creamy spiced mussels

Fresh mussels are surprisingly quick and easy to prepare. Serve this dish with bread to mop up the delicious juices.

TAKES 35 MINUTES • SERVES 4

2kg/4lb 8oz fresh mussels
150ml/¼ pint dry white wine
2 shallots, finely chopped
25g/1oz butter
1 tsp plain flour
1–2 tsp curry paste
100g/3½oz crème fraîche
chopped parsley, to serve

1 Scrub the mussels in a large bowl of cold water and discard any that are open. Put in a large pan with the wine. Bring to the boil, cover and shake the pan over a high heat until the mussels are open – about 3–4 minutes.
2 Tip the mussels into a colander set over a large bowl to catch the juices. Discard any that have not opened. Strain the cooking liquid through a sieve. Keep the mussels warm.
3 Fry the shallots in the butter in the large pan until softened. Stir in the flour and curry paste and cook for 1 minute. Add the cooking liquid (except the last little bit, which may be gritty) and season with pepper, but no salt.
4 Stir in the crème fraîche and warm over a low heat until thick and glossy. Divide the mussels among four bowls and pour over the sauce. Scatter with parsley and serve.

PER SERVING 285 kcals, protein 19g, carbs 6g, fat 18g, sat fat 10g, fibre 1g, added sugar none, salt 1.27g

Cheesy fish grills

Italian-style roasted fish

Zesty roast salmon and cod

Roasting is a foolproof way of cooking fish. In this recipe the fish stays moist and the peppers become soft and sweet.

TAKES ABOUT 1 HOUR (OR LONGER, DEPENDING ON MARINATING) • SERVES 8

800g/1lb 12oz thick skinless salmon fillet, cut into 8
800g/1lb 12oz thick skinless sustainably caught cod loin, cut into 8
85g/3oz raisins
3 tbsp olive oil
zest and juice 2 oranges
3 red peppers, halved, deseeded and cut into 6
3 orange peppers, halved, deseeded and cut into 6
50g/2oz toasted pine nuts
large handful of flat-leaf parsley, roughly chopped, to garnish

1 Place the fish and raisins in a large bowl, add 2 tablespoons olive oil and the orange zest and juice, and season well. Carefully toss the fish to coat, cover, and leave to marinate for 30 minutes or up to 2 hours. Heat the oven to 200C/180C fan/gas 6.
2 Meanwhile, place the peppers in a large, shallow roasting tin and drizzle with the remaining olive oil. Season, toss together and roast in the oven for 30 minutes.
3 Arrange the fish and raisins on top of the peppers and pour over the juices. Scatter the pine nuts over and season with a good pinch of salt. Cook in the oven for 12–15 minutes until the fish is just cooked through. Scatter with parsley and bring to the table.

PER SERVING 407 kcals, protein 41g, carbs 15g, fat 21g, sat fat 3g, fibre 2g, added sugar none, salt 0.3g

Creamy spiced mussels

Fresh mussels are surprisingly quick and easy to prepare. Serve this dish with bread to mop up the delicious juices.

TAKES 35 MINUTES • SERVES 4

2kg/4lb 8oz fresh mussels
150ml/¼ pint dry white wine
2 shallots, finely chopped
25g/1oz butter
1 tsp plain flour
1–2 tsp curry paste
100g/3½oz crème fraîche
chopped parsley, to serve

1 Scrub the mussels in a large bowl of cold water and discard any that are open. Put in a large pan with the wine. Bring to the boil, cover and shake the pan over a high heat until the mussels are open – about 3–4 minutes.
2 Tip the mussels into a colander set over a large bowl to catch the juices. Discard any that have not opened. Strain the cooking liquid through a sieve. Keep the mussels warm.
3 Fry the shallots in the butter in the large pan until softened. Stir in the flour and curry paste and cook for 1 minute. Add the cooking liquid (except the last little bit, which may be gritty) and season with pepper, but no salt.
4 Stir in the crème fraîche and warm over a low heat until thick and glossy. Divide the mussels among four bowls and pour over the sauce. Scatter with parsley and serve.

PER SERVING 285 kcals, protein 19g, carbs 6g, fat 18g, sat fat 10g, fibre 1g, added sugar none, salt 1.27g

Creamy spiced mussels

Zesty roast salmon and cod

Rich paprika seafood bowl

One-pots can be so good for you: this stew counts as three of your 5-a-day and it's low in fat.

TAKES 30 MINUTES • SERVES 4

2 tbsp olive oil
2 onions, halved and thinly sliced
2 celery sticks, finely chopped
1 large bunch flat-leaf parsley, leaves and
    stalks separated
2–3 tsp paprika
200g/7oz roasted red peppers from a jar,
    drained weight, thickly sliced
400g can chopped tomatoes with garlic
400g/12oz white fish fillet, cut into very large
    chunks
few fresh mussels (optional)
lightly toasted bread, to serve

1 Heat half the oil in a pan, then add the onions, celery and a little salt. Cover, then gently fry until soft, about 10 minutes.
2 Put the parsley stalks, half the leaves, remaining oil and seasoning into a food processor, and whizz to a paste. Add this and the paprika to the softened onions, frying for a few minutes. Tip in the peppers and tomatoes with a splash of water, then simmer for 10 minutes until the sauce has reduced.
3 Lay the fish and mussels, if using, on top of the sauce, put a lid on, then simmer for 5 minutes until the fish is just flaking and the mussels have opened – discard any that stay shut. Gently stir the seafood into the sauce, season, then serve in bowls with some lightly toasted bread.

PER SERVING 192 kcals, protein 22g, carbs 12g, fat 7g, sat fat 1g, fibre 4g, sugar 8g, salt 1.14g

Scallops with chilli and lime

Try this as a starter for a special meal for two.

TAKES 10–15 MINUTES • SERVES 2

2 tbsp olive oil
10 scallops
2 large garlic cloves, chopped
2 tsp chopped fresh red chilli
juice 1 lime
small handful of coriander, roughly chopped

1 Heat the oil in a non-stick frying pan until hot, add the scallops and pan fry for 1 minute until golden underneath. Flip them over and sprinkle with the garlic and chilli.
2 Cook for 1 minute more, then pour over the lime juice and season with salt and pepper. Serve immediately, scattered with the coriander.

PER SERVING 260 kcals, protein 34g, carbs 2g, fat 13g, sat fat 2g, fibre 0.3g, added sugar none, salt 0.99g

Rich paprika seafood bowl

Scallops with chilli and lime

One-pan salmon with roast asparagus

This fresh one-pan recipe is really two recipes in one – for an easy side dish to complement a spring roast, just cook it without the fish.

TAKES 1 HOUR 20 MINUTES • SERVES 2

400g/14oz new potatoes, halved if large
2 tbsp olive oil
8 asparagus spears, trimmed and halved
2 handfuls cherry tomatoes
1 tbsp balsamic vinegar
2 salmon fillets, about 140g/5oz each
handful of fresh basil leaves, to garnish

1 Heat the oven to 220C/200C fan/gas 7. Tip the potatoes and 1 tablespoon of olive oil into an ovenproof dish, then roast the potatoes for 20 minutes until just starting to brown.
2 Toss the asparagus in with the potatoes, then return to the oven for 15 minutes. Throw in the cherry tomatoes and vinegar, and nestle the salmon among the vegetables. Drizzle with the remaining oil and return to the oven for a final 10–15 minutes until the salmon is cooked through. Scatter over the basil leaves and serve everything scooped straight from the dish.

PER SERVING 483 kcals, protein 33g, carbs 34g, fat 25g, sat fat 4g, fibre 3g, sugar 6g, salt 0.24g

Spanish fish stew

Use any sustainably caught white fish or salmon fillets in this recipe – perfect mopped up with crusty bread.

TAKES 50 MINUTES • SERVES 4

handful of flat-leaf parsley leaves, chopped zest and juice 1 lemon
2 garlic cloves, finely chopped
3 tbsp olive oil, plus extra to drizzle
1 medium onion, finely sliced
500g/1lb 2oz floury potatoes, cut into small cubes
1 tsp paprika
pinch of cayenne pepper
400g can chopped tomatoes
1 fish stock cube, crumbled
200g/7oz raw peeled king prawns
½ x 410g can chickpeas, drained and rinsed
500g/1lb 2oz skinless fish fillets, cut into very large chunks

1 In a small bowl, mix the parsley with the lemon zest and half the garlic, then set aside. Heat 2 tablespoons oil in a large sauté pan. Add the onion and potatoes, cover and cook for 5 minutes until the onion has softened. Add the remaining oil and garlic and the spices, then cook for 2 minutes more.
2 Pour over the lemon juice, sizzle for a few seconds, then add the tomatoes, half a can of water and the stock cube. Season, cover, and simmer for 15–20 minutes until the potatoes are just cooked.
3 Stir through the prawns and chickpeas, then nestle the fish into the top of the stew. Reduce the heat, re-cover, then cook for about 8 minutes, stirring very gently once or twice. Scatter with the parsley mix and drizzle with a little olive oil to serve.

PER SERVING 382 kcals, protein 39g, carbs 33g, fat 11g, sat fat 2g, fibre 5g, sugar 5g, salt 1.92g

One-pan salmon with roast asparagus

Spanish fish stew

Steamed mussels with leeks, thyme and bacon

For this dish, try to buy the smallest mussels you can find; they will always be the sweetest.

TAKES 35 MINUTES • SERVES 2

750g/1lb 10oz mussels
25g/1oz butter
6 rashers smoked streaky bacon, chopped
   into small pieces
2 small leeks, sliced on the diagonal
handful of fresh thyme sprigs
1 small glass cider or white wine
crusty bread, to serve

1 Scrub and de-beard the mussels. Heat half the butter in a pan, then sizzle the bacon for 3–4 minutes until starting to brown. Add the leeks and thyme, then gently fry everything together for 4–5 minutes until soft.
2 Turn the heat up high, add the mussels and cider or wine, then cover and cook for 4–5 minutes, shaking the pan occasionally, until the mussels have opened. Discard any that don't open.
3 Scoop the mussels and the other solid bits into a dish, then place the pan back on the heat. Boil the juices for 1 minute with the rest of the butter, then pour over the mussels and serve with crusty bread.

PER SERVING 377 kcals, protein 24g, carbs 9g, fat 26g, sat fat 12g, fibre 2g, sugar 5g, salt 2.76g

Smoked salmon and lemon risotto

Smoked salmon is no more costly than cooking with red meat and adds a touch of luxury to this simple weeknight supper.

TAKES 25 MINUTES • SERVES 4

1 onion, finely chopped
2 tbsp olive oil
350g/12oz risotto rice, such as arborio
1 garlic clove, finely chopped
1½ litres/2¾ pints boiling vegetable stock
170g pack smoked salmon, three-quarters
   chopped
85g/3oz reduced-fat mascarpone
3 tbsp flat-leaf parsley, chopped
grated zest of 1 lemon, plus squeeze of juice
   (optional), to taste
handful of rocket leaves, to serve

1 Fry the onion in the oil over a medium heat for 5 minutes. Add the rice and garlic, then cook for 2 minutes, stirring continuously. Pour in the stock a ladleful at a time, stirring, until almost all the stock has been absorbed and the rice is cooked and creamy.
2 Remove from the heat and add the chopped salmon, mascarpone, parsley and lemon zest. Grind in some black pepper, but don't add salt as the salmon will be salty enough. Leave for 5 minutes to settle, then taste and add a little lemon juice, if you like. Serve topped with the reserved salmon (roughly torn) and some rocket leaves.

PER SERVING 500 kcals, protein 21g, carbs 75g, fat 15g, sat fat 5g, fibre 4g, sugar 5g, salt 2.58g

Smoked salmon and lemon risotto

Steamed mussels with leeks, thyme and bacon

Lemon and rosemary crusted fish fillets

Pressing a layer of breadcrumbs on to fish not only adds crunch but also helps to cook it to perfection, protecting it from the direct heat of the grill. The crumbs can be made using any green herbs.

TAKES 20 MINUTES • SERVES 4

4 sustainably caught white fish fillets
2 fresh rosemary sprigs, leaves chopped, or
    1 tsp dried
50g/2oz bread (about 2 slices), torn into pieces
zest 2 lemons, plus wedges to serve
1 tbsp olive oil

1 Heat the grill to medium. Place the fish fillets, skin-side up, on a baking sheet, then grill for 4 minutes.
2 Meanwhile, place the rosemary, bread, lemon zest and some seasoning in a food processor, then blitz to make fine crumbs.
3 Turn the fish over, then press the crumbs over the top of each fillet. Drizzle with olive oil, then grill for 4 minutes until the crust is golden and the fish is cooked through and just flaking. Serve with lemon wedges for squeezing over.

PER SERVING 184 kcals, protein 26g, carbs 6g, fat 6g, sat fat 1g, fibre none, sugar none, salt 0.51g

Chilli prawn noodles

This is a light and aromatic dish made entirely from storecupboard ingredients, making it a great recipe to have in reserve for when you haven't had time to pop to the shops.

TAKES 30–40 MINUTES • SERVES 4

2 tbsp olive oil
1 onion, roughly chopped
1 heaped tbsp coriander purée (from a tube)
pinch of dried chilli flakes, or to taste
400g can chopped tomatoes with garlic
1 heaped tbsp tomato purée
1 tbsp vegetable bouillon powder
150g pack straight-to-wok noodles
400g/14oz frozen prawns (large North Atlantic
    ones are tender and juicy)
sugar (optional)

1 Heat the oil in a wok or deep frying pan. Toss in the onion, squeeze in the coriander purée and sprinkle over the chilli flakes to taste (go easy at this stage). Stir fry for 5 minutes until the onion is softened but not browned.
2 Pour in the tomatoes and 1½ canfuls hot water, add the tomato purée and sprinkle over the bouillon powder. Season well. Bring to a bubble, stirring, then lower the heat and let the sauce simmer gently for about 15 minutes until slightly reduced but still runny.
3 When the sauce is ready, tip in the noodles and frozen prawns. Stir well and heat through for 2 minutes only – just to defrost the prawns and heat through the noodles. Taste for seasoning before serving, and add more chilli flakes and a little sugar, if you like.

PER SERVING 228 kcals, protein 22g, carbs 18g, fat 8g, sat fat 0.8g, fibre 2.1g, added sugar none, salt 2.95g

Lemon and rosemary crusted fish fillets

Chilli prawn noodles

Tilapia in Thai sauce

This is a popular way to serve fish in Thailand. The only difference is they deep-fry the fish; here we've kept everything in one pan.

TAKES 30 MINUTES • SERVES 2

4 tilapia fillets (or choose any sustainably
    caught white fish)
2 tbsp cornflour
2 tbsp sunflower oil
4 spring onions, sliced
2 garlic cloves, crushed
small knob of ginger, finely chopped
2 tbsp soy sauce
1 tbsp brown sugar
juice 1 lime, plus 1 lime chopped into wedges,
    to serve
1 red chilli, deseeded and sliced and handful
    of Thai basil or coriander leaves, to garnish

1 Coat the fish fillets in the cornflour. Heat the oil in a large non-stick frying pan, sizzle the fillets for 2–3 minutes on each side until crisp, then remove and keep warm.
2 In the same pan, briefly fry the spring onions, garlic and ginger, then add the soy sauce, brown sugar and lime juice, and simmer until slightly syrupy. Spoon the sauce over the fish, scatter with the chilli and Thai basil or coriander, then serve with the lime wedges on the side.

PER SERVING 328 kcals, protein 28g, carbs 25g, fat 14g, sat fat 2g, fibre 1g, sugar 10g, salt 2.94g

Super-fast prawn noodles

Medium or thick udon-style noodles work best in this recipe. Serve with a spoon so you can slurp up all the soupy stock.

TAKES 15 MINUTES • SERVES 4

1 litre/1¾ pints chicken stock
2 tbsp oyster sauce
2 tbsp hoisin sauce
1 tbsp fish sauce
large knob of ginger, shredded into thin
    matchsticks
300g/10oz peeled king prawns (raw would be
    best, but cooked are fine)
4 bok choi, each cut into quarters
2 sachets straight-to-wok noodles
4 spring onions, finely sliced, to garnish

1 In a wok or large pan, bring the stock to the boil. Stir the sauces into the stock, then add the ginger. Simmer for a moment, then add the prawns; if raw, simmer for 2 minutes until they turn pink before adding the bok choi; if cooked, add together with the bok choi and cook for 2 minutes until just wilted.
2 Slip the noodles into the broth and stir them gently to loosen. Bring the liquid back to a simmer and cook for 2 minutes more to warm them through. Scatter with spring onions and serve straight from the wok, using tongs for the noodles and a ladle for the broth.

PER SERVING 277 kcals, protein 29g, carbs 33g, fat 4g, sat fat none, fibre 2g, sugar 6g, salt 3.82g

Super-fast prawn noodles

Tilapia in Thai sauce

Friday-night fish with chorizo and new potatoes

This makes a wonderful end-of-week supper to share. The sherry adds steam to the pan and cooks the potatoes.

TAKES 30 MINUTES • SERVES 2

1 tbsp extra-virgin olive oil, plus extra to drizzle
50g/2oz chorizo, peeled and thinly sliced
450g/1lb salad or new potatoes, sliced (we used Charlotte)
4 tbsp dry sherry (more if you need it)
2 skinless thick white fish fillets (we used sustainably-caught haddock)
good handful of cherry tomatoes, halved
20g pack flat-leaf parsley, leaves chopped
crusty bread, to serve

1 Heat a large lidded frying pan, then add the oil. Tip in the chorizo, fry for 2 minutes until it starts to release its oils, then tip in the potatoes and some seasoning. Splash over 3 tablespoons sherry, cover the pan tightly, then leave to cook for 10–15 minutes until the potatoes are just tender. Move them around the pan a bit halfway through.
2 Season the fish well. Give the potatoes another stir, add the cherry tomatoes and most of the chopped parsley to the pan, then lay the fish on top. Splash over 1 tablespoon sherry, put the lid on again, then leave to cook for 5 minutes, or until the fish has turned white and is flaky when prodded in the middle. Scatter the whole dish with a little more parsley and drizzle with more extra-virgin oil. Serve straight away with crusty bread.

PER SERVING 534 kcals, protein 47g, carbs 39g, fat 19g, sat fat 4g, fibre 3g, sugar 5g, salt 0.79g

Easy Thai prawn curry

One you've tried this can't-go-wrong curry you'll make it again and again. Frozen prawns are better value and are often in better condition than fresh.

TAKES 20 MINUTES • SERVES 4

1 tbsp vegetable oil
1 onion, chopped
1 tsp grated ginger
1–2 tsp Thai red curry paste
400g can chopped tomatoes
50g sachet creamed coconut
400g/14oz frozen raw peeled prawns
chopped fresh coriander leaves, to garnish

1 Heat the oil in a medium saucepan. Tip in the onion and ginger, then cook for a few minutes until softened. Stir in the curry paste, then cook for 1 minute more. Pour over the chopped tomatoes and stir in the creamed coconut. Bring to the boil, then leave to simmer for 5 minutes, adding a little boiling water if the mixture gets too thick.
2 Tip in the prawns, then cook for around 5–10 minutes more, depending on how large they are. Sprinkle with coriander to serve.

PER SERVING 180 kcals, protein 20g, carbs 6g, fat 9g, sat fat 4g, fibre 1g, sugar 5g, salt 0.86g

Friday-night fish with chorizo and new potatoes

Easy Thai prawn curry

Smoked haddock stovies

Hearty and healthy, this is comfort food at its best – ideal for a mid-week supper in the winter.

TAKES 30–40 MINUTES • SERVES 4

knob of butter
splash of vegetable oil
2 onions, thinly sliced
1kg/2lb 4oz floury potatoes, such as Maris Piper
    or King Edward, peeled and thickly sliced
500g/1lb 2oz skinless smoked haddock,
    cut into large chunks
handful of parsley, coarsely chopped, to garnish

1 Heat the butter and oil in a large wide pan, add the onions and cook for 5 minutes, stirring until lightly coloured. Tip in the potatoes and cook for a further 5 minutes, stirring often, until they are also lightly coloured.
2 Pour in 425ml/¾ pint water and grind in black pepper to taste. Stir to mix, then gently stir in the fish and bring to the boil. Cover and cook for 10 minutes or until the potatoes and fish are tender. Scatter with parsley before serving.

PER SERVING 307 kcals, protein 29g, carbs 39g, fat 5g, sat fat 2g, fibre 4g, added sugar none, salt 2.5g

Creamy haddock and tatties

This must be the easiest fish pie ever! There are only five ingredients and three simple steps, and the finished dish is very tasty indeed.

TAKES 15–20 MINUTES • SERVES 2

400g/14oz smoked haddock (undyed is best,
    but not essential), skinned and chopped into
    chunks
1 trimmed leek, finely sliced
handful of parsley, chopped
142ml pot double cream
2 medium baking potatoes, about 200g/7oz
    each, unpeeled, sliced as thinly as possible

1 Scatter the haddock, leek and parsley over the base of a shallow microwave dish and mix together with your fingers or a spoon. Drizzle over half the cream and 5 tablespoons water. Lay the potato slices over the fish and leek. Season with a little salt and plenty of black pepper, and drizzle over the remaining cream.
2 Cover the dish with cling film and pierce a few times. Microwave on High for 8–10 minutes until everything is bubbling away and the potatoes are tender when pierced with a knife. While the dish is in the microwave, heat the grill to high.
3 Remove the cling film and put the dish under the grill until the potatoes are golden. Leave to stand for a minute or two before serving.

PER SERVING 646 kcals, protein 45g, carbs 38g, fat 36g, sat fat 22g, fibre 4g, added sugar none, salt 3.97g

Smoked haddock stovies

Creamy haddock and tatties

Smoked salmon and celeriac bake

This is a Sweden-inspired, rich supper dish using easily available ingredients.

TAKES ABOUT 2 HOURS • SERVES 6

juice 1 lemon
1 small celeriac, about 650g/1lb 7oz
2 medium baking potatoes
2 x 125g packs sliced smoked salmon
small handful of dill, chopped
1 onion, finely sliced
284ml pot double cream

1 Heat the oven to 200C/180C fan/gas 6. Pour the lemon juice into a large bowl. Peel and quarter the celeriac, cut into slices the thickness of a £1 coin and toss into the lemon juice. Peel and thinly slice the potatoes and toss with the celeriac.
2 Layer the celeriac, potatoes and salmon slices in a large ovenproof dish, sprinkling dill, onion and cream over each layer, together with a little salt and plenty of black pepper. You should have three layers of vegetables with two layers of salmon, onion and dill. Finish with the remaining cream.
3 Cover the dish with foil, place on a baking sheet and bake for 45 minutes. Uncover and bake for 30–40 minutes more, until the vegetables feel tender when pierced and the top is golden. Cool slightly before serving.

PER SERVING 328 kcals, protein 14g, carbs 13g, fat 25g, sat fat 15g, fibre 3g, added sugar none, salt 2.19g

Spicy prawn and chorizo rice

An ever-popular recipe for an easy and delicious one-pot meal.

TAKES 45–55 MINUTES • SERVES 6

2 tbsp olive oil
2 garlic cloves, finely chopped
1 large onion, finely chopped
2 red chillies, deseeded and chopped
400g/14oz chorizo sausage, skinned and cut into chunks
450g/1lb long-grain rice
1 tsp smoked paprika
200ml/7fl oz dry white wine
1.5 litres/2¾ pints hot chicken stock (if using cubes, don't use more than 2)
175g/6oz frozen broad beans or peas
400g/14oz raw shelled tiger prawns, thawed if frozen
250g/9oz cherry tomatoes, halved
3 tbsp chopped flat-leaf parsley, plus extra for sprinkling

1 Heat the oil in a wide shallow pan and fry the garlic, onion, chillies and chorizo for a few minutes until the onion has softened. Stir in the rice and paprika, then add the wine and bubble away until it evaporates.
2 Pour in the stock, lower the heat and cook gently for 10 minutes, stirring occasionally. Tip in the beans or peas, season and cook for 7–10 minutes, stirring, until the rice is tender. Keep some boiling water at the ready in case you need it to keep the rice moist.
3 Stir in the prawns and tomatoes and cook for a few minutes until the prawns turn pink. Toss in the parsley and taste for seasoning before serving, sprinkled with a little more parsley.

PER SERVING 624 kcals, protein 33g, carbs 75g, fat 21g, sat fat 1g, fibre 3g, added sugar none, salt 2.15g

Fish O'leekie

Accurate microwave timings ensure that everything is cooked together perfectly.

TAKES 20–30 MINUTES • SERVES 4

1 leek, finely sliced
100g/3½oz smoked lean back bacon, chopped
500ml/18fl oz vegetable stock
300g/10oz American easy-cook rice
500g/1lb 2oz cod or haddock fillet, skinned
 and cut into large chunks
3 tbsp chopped fresh parsley
grated zest and juice 1 lemon

1 Put the leek and bacon in a medium microwave dish with 4 tablespoons of the stock. Cover the dish with cling film, pierce the film with a knife and microwave on High for 5 minutes.
2 Uncover the dish and stir the rice and remaining stock into the leek and bacon. Microwave on High for a further 5 minutes.
3 Gently stir in the fish chunks, cover the dish with cling film again, pierce the film with a knife and cook for a further 10 minutes until the fish and rice are done.
4 Stir in the parsley and lemon zest and juice. Leave to stand for 2–3 minutes before serving.

PER SERVING 437 kcals, protein 35g, carbs 66g, fat 6g, sat fat 1g, fibre 1g, added sugar none, salt 1.8g

Prawn pilau

You can use cooked, chopped chicken instead of the prawns, if you prefer.

TAKES 25–30 MINUTES • SERVES 4

2 tbsp korma curry paste
1 small onion, finely chopped
300g/10oz basmati rice, rinsed and drained
700ml/1¼ pints chicken stock
150g pack cooked peeled prawns, defrosted
 if frozen
cupful of frozen peas
1 red chilli, deseeded and sliced into rings
handful of coriander leaves, chopped, and
 lemon wedges, to serve

1 Heat a large wide pan and dry fry the curry paste with the onion for 4–5 minutes until the onion begins to soften. Add the rice to the pan and stir to coat in the curry paste. Add the stock, then bring to the boil.
2 Cover the pan and turn the heat down to low. Leave the rice to simmer slowly for 12–15 minutes until the liquid has been absorbed and the rice is cooked. Turn off the heat and stir in the prawns, peas and chilli. Cover the pan and leave to stand for 5 minutes.
3 Fluff up the rice grains with a fork and season if you want. Scatter over the coriander and serve with lemon wedges.

PER SERVING 340 kcals, protein 18g, carbs 65g, fat 3g, sat fat 1g, fibre 2g, added sugar none, salt 2.38g

Potato and mozzarella tortilla, page 125

Veggie-friendly dishes

Mexican bean salad

This filling and balanced salad really will hit the spot with lots of texture and taste – and that all-important spicy kick.

TAKES 20 MINUTES • SERVES 4

4 eggs
2 avocados, peeled and stoned
2 x 400g cans beans (we used kidney beans
    and pinto beans), drained and rinsed
1 small red onion, finely sliced
1 large bunch fresh coriander, leaves only,
    roughly chopped
250g punnet cherry tomatoes, halved
3 tbsp good-quality shop-bought dressing (try
    one with lime and coriander)
1 red chilli, deseeded and finely sliced
½ tsp ground cumin

1 Lower the eggs into a pan of boiling water and boil for 6½ minutes, then cool under running water.
2 Slice the avocados and place them in a large bowl with the beans, onion, coriander and tomatoes. Tip in the dressing, chilli and cumin, and toss well.
3 Once the eggs are just warm, peel off the shells and cut into quarters. Nestle the eggs into the salad and serve straight away.

PER SERVING 430 kcals, protein 20g, carbs 25g, fat 29g, sat fat 3g, fibre 10g, sugar 6g, salt 1.61g

Mushroom stroganoff on toast

Mushrooms in a creamy sauce make the perfect quick fix, served on wholegrain toast. Choose chestnut mushrooms over white ones as they have a much deeper flavour.

TAKES 10 MINUTES • SERVES 2

25g/1oz ready-made garlic butter (or mix
    25g/1oz butter with 1 crushed garlic clove),
    plus a little extra for spreading
250g pack chestnut mushrooms, thickly sliced
2 thick slices granary bread
1 tsp wholegrain mustard
5 tbsp soured cream or crème fraîche
few snipped fresh chives or spring onion tops

1 Tip the butter into a pan then, when sizzling, add the mushrooms and cook over a high heat, stirring occasionally until the mushrooms are tender and juicy.
2 Meanwhile, toast and lightly butter the bread and put on two plates. Stir the mustard and some salt and pepper into the mushrooms along with 4 tablespoons of the soured cream or crème fraîche. When lightly mixed, pile the mushrooms and their creamy sauce on the toast. Spoon the last of the soured cream or crème fraîche on top, snip over the chives or spring onions and grind over some black pepper.

PER SERVING 322 kcals, protein 8g, carbs 21g, fat 24g, sat fat 14g, fibre 3g, added sugar none, salt 1.08g

Mushroom stroganoff on toast

Mexican bean salad

Deep-dish cheese, onion and potato pie

Food doesn't get much heartier, or fun to make, than this big, comforting cheese pie. Great with a simple salad.

TAKES 2 HOURS, PLUS RESTING TIME
• SERVES 6

200g/7oz strong hard cheese,
    ½ coarsely grated, ½ cut into small chunks
200g pot crème fraîche
500g/1lb 2oz shortcrust pastry
1kg/2lb 4oz floury potatoes, thinly sliced
2 onions, finely sliced
1 bunch spring onions, roughly chopped
small pinch of grated nutmeg
large pinch of paprika
1 egg, beaten

1 Heat the oven to 200C/180C fan/gas 6. Mix the grated cheese with the crème fraîche. Grease and lightly flour a pie dish or shallow cake tin about 23cm wide. Roll out two-thirds of the pastry on a floured surface until large enough to line the tin.
2 Layer the potatoes, onions, spring onions and chunks of cheese with splodges of the crème fraîche mix, seasoning with some black pepper and the nutmeg and paprika as you go. The filling will come up way above the pastry.
3 Roll the remaining pastry so it fits over the filling. Brush the sides with egg, lay the pastry over, then trim with a knife. Crimp the sides, brush all over with egg then bake on a baking sheet for 30 minutes. Reduce the oven to 180C/160C fan/gas 4, then bake for 1 hour more. Rest the pie for 10 minutes, then slice.

PER SERVING 820 kcals, protein 20g, carbs 73g, fat 52g, sat fat 26g, fibre 5g, sugar 5g, salt 1.53g

Cheesy baked onions

Make onions into a meal with a simple cheesy stuffing and a salad on the side.

TAKES 35 MINUTES • SERVES 4

4 large onions, peeled
½ x 150g ball reduced-fat mozzarella, roughly
    chopped
85g/3oz Cheddar, grated
2 tbsp pitted olives, halved
50g/2oz roasted red peppers from a jar, drained
    and roughly chopped
1 garlic clove, crushed
50g/2oz breadcrumbs
leaves from a few fresh thyme sprigs

1 Heat the oven to 220C/200C fan/gas 7. Halve each onion through the middle. Microwave in a baking dish in pairs for around 4 minutes on High until soft. Remove the middles of the onions, leaving about three outer layers in place, like little bowls.
2 Whizz the onion middles in a food processor until pulpy. Mix with the mozzarella, half of the Cheddar, the olives, peppers, garlic, breadcrumbs and most of the thyme, then season well. Spoon the filling into the onion cases and return to the baking dish. Sprinkle with the remaining Cheddar and thyme, then roast for 15 minutes until hot through and lightly golden.

PER SERVING 255 kcals, protein 13g, carbs 27g, fat 11g, sat fat 6g, fibre 4g, sugar 12g, salt 1.16g

Deep-dish cheese, onion and potato pie

Cheesy baked onions

Indian chickpea and vegetable soup

Warm up lunchtimes with a bowl of gently spiced soup that's great with naan bread. If you're more into Italian flavours, swap the ginger and garam masala for 1 tablespoon of chopped rosemary.

TAKES 30 MINUTES • SERVES 4

1 tbsp vegetable oil
1 large onion, chopped
1 tsp finely grated ginger
1 garlic clove, chopped
1 tbsp garam masala
850ml/1½ pints vegetable stock
2 large carrots, quartered lengthways and
    chopped
400g/14oz can chickpeas, drained and rinsed
100g/3½oz green beans, chopped

1 Heat the oil in a medium pan, then add the onion, ginger and garlic. Fry for 2 minutes, then add the garam masala; give it 1 minute more, then add the stock and carrots. Simmer for 15 minutes, then add the chickpeas.
2 Use a stick blender to whizz the soup a little. Stir in the beans, simmer for 3 minutes, then divide among bowls and serve.

PER SERVING 168 kcals, protein 7g, carbs 23g, fat 6g, sat fat none, fibre 6g, sugar 10g, salt 0.66g

Spring vegetable soup with basil pesto

Soup can be both satisfying and special, as this dish proves.

TAKES 25 MINUTES • SERVES 2 (EASILY DOUBLED)

1 tbsp olive oil
2 leeks, washed and chopped
100g/3½oz green beans, halved
1 large courgette, diced
1.2 litres/2 pints hot vegetable stock
3 vine-ripened tomatoes, deseeded and
    chopped
400g can cannellini beans, drained and rinsed
1 nest vermicelli pasta, about 25g/1oz
crusty bread, to serve
FOR THE PESTO
25g pack fresh basil
1 garlic clove, crushed
25g/1oz pistachio or pine nuts
25g/1oz Parmesan or vegetarian
    Parmesan-style cheese, grated
2 tbsp olive oil

1 Heat the oil, then fry the leeks until softened. Add the green beans and courgette, then pour in the stock and season to taste. Cover and simmer for 5 minutes.
2 Meanwhile, make the pesto. Put the basil, garlic, nuts, cheese, oil and ½ teaspoon salt in a food processor, then blitz until smooth.
3 Stir the tomatoes, cannellini beans and vermicelli into the soup pan, then simmer for 5 minutes more until the veg are just tender.
4 Stir in half of the pesto. Ladle the soup into bowls and serve with the rest of the pesto spooned on top. Eat with chunks of crusty bread on the side.

PER SERVING 594 kcals, protein 27g, carbs 56g, fat 31g, sat fat 6g, fibre 16g, sugar 19g, salt 2.35g

Potato and mozzarella tortilla

Use your own potato leftovers, if you like. Serve with a peppery rocket and watercress salad.

TAKES 30 MINUTES • SERVES 6

2 tbsp olive oil
2 x 400g packs ready-roasted potatoes
 (available with different flavourings from
 most supermarkets)
8 eggs, beaten
4 vine-ripened tomatoes, sliced
150g ball mozzarella, torn into pieces

1 Heat the oil in a large frying pan. Empty the potatoes into the pan, spread them out to cover the base, then fry for 5 minutes. Pour in the beaten eggs so they completely cover the potatoes, season well and leave the tortilla to cook on a medium heat for about 15–20 minutes, or until the base and edges have set.
2 Meanwhile Heat the grill to high. Take the tortilla off the hob and place under the grill until the top is firm, then remove from the grill and scatter over the tomatoes and mozzarella. Put the tortilla back under the grill for a further 3–5 minutes, or until the tomatoes are soft and the cheese has melted. Serve, cut into thick wedges.

PER SERVING 465 kcals, protein 28g, carbs 23g, fat 32g, sat fat 7g, fibre 3g, added sugar none, salt 0.72g

Greek salad omelette

Juicy tomatoes and creamy cheese ensure a dish with flavours that will burst in your mouth.

TAKES 15–20 MINUTES • SERVES 4–6

10 eggs
handful of parsley leaves, chopped
2 tbsp olive oil
1 large red onion, cut into wedges
3 tomatoes, chopped into large chunks
large handful of black olives (pitted are easier
 to eat)
100g/3½oz feta, crumbled

1 Heat the grill to high. Whisk the eggs in a large bowl with the chopped parsley, pepper, and salt if you want. Heat the oil in a large, non-stick frying pan, then fry the onion wedges over a high heat for about 4 minutes until they start to brown around the edges. Add the tomatoes and olives, stir and cook for 1–2 minutes until the tomatoes begin to soften.
2 Turn the heat down to medium and pour in the eggs. Stir the eggs as they begin to set, until half cooked but still runny in places – about 2 minutes. Scatter over the feta, then slide the pan under the grill for 5–6 minutes until the omelette is puffed up and golden. Cut into wedges and serve straight from the pan.

PER SERVING for four 371 kcals, protein 24g, carbs 5g, fat 28g, sat fat 9g, fibre 1g, added sugar none, salt 2g

Shallot tarte Tatin

This special dish can be relished by everyone, whether vegetarian or not. If you want to make it ahead, it will sit in the fridge, ready to bake, for a day or two.

TAKES 1 HOUR • SERVES 4

2 tbsp olive oil
25g/1oz butter
500g/1lb 2oz shallots, peeled and halved
2 tbsp balsamic vinegar
1 tbsp fresh thyme leaves, or 2 tsp dried
300g/10oz puff pastry, defrosted if frozen
    and cut into two
100g/3½oz grated Cheddar or Emmental

1 Heat the oil and butter in a frying pan, add the shallots and fry gently for 10 minutes until softened and lightly browned. Stir in the vinegar, thyme and 1 tablespoon water; cook for 5 minutes, stirring occasionally. Tip into a shallow non-stick cake or pie tin, roughly 20cm wide. Leave to cool.
2 Heat the oven to 200C/180C fan/gas 6. Roll out each piece of pastry to about 5cm larger than the top of the cake tin. Put one piece over the shallots. Sprinkle evenly with cheese then cover with the second piece. Trim the pastry to a little larger than the tin, then tuck the edges down between the shallots and the side of the tin.
3 Bake for 25–30 minutes until the pastry is crisp and golden. Cool in the tin for around 5 minutes, turn out on to a flat plate, cut into wedges and serve warm.

PER SERVING 510 kcals, protein 13g, carbs 33g, fat 37g, sat fat 17g, fibre 2g, sugar 6g, salt 1.18g

Fennel with tomatoes and white wine

Try something different and tuck into a plateful of beautifully simple fennel and tomatoes. Serve with some goat's cheese, if you like, and scoop the whole lot up with crusty bread.

TAKES 1 HOUR 20 MINUTES • SERVES 2 AS A MAIN OR 4 AS A STARTER 1

4 fennel bulbs
2 tbsp fruity olive oil
2 garlic cloves, crushed
a generous pinch of crushed dried chilli
1 tbsp chopped fresh thyme leaves
4 ripe tomatoes, skinned and roughly chopped
150ml/¼ pint dry white wine
100ml/3½fl oz vegetable stock (a cube is fine)
a pinch of caster sugar (optional)
1 tbsp chopped flat-leaf parsley, to garnish

1 Heat the oven to 180C/160C fan/gas 4. Trim the fennel and cut into quarters through the root. (You may need to cut larger ones in half, then into thirds so they all cook evenly.) Heat the oil in a roasting pan on the hob, add the fennel and cook until golden brown on all sides. Remove from the pan.
2 Fry the garlic, chilli and thyme for about 30 seconds, add the tomatoes and cook for a further 3 minutes. Add the wine and bring to the boil. Simmer for 1 minute, add the stock, bring back to the boil and simmer for 2–3 minutes.
3 Season the tomato mix, adding a pinch of sugar, if needed, then add the fennel and spoon the sauce over it. Cover with foil and cook in the oven for 1 hour or until the fennel is tender. Scatter with the parsley and serve.

PER SERVING 110 kcals, protein 2g, carbs 6g, fat 6g, sat fat 1g, fibre 4g, added sugar none, salt 0.2g

Shallot tarte Tatin

Fennel with tomatoes and white wine

Easy ratatouille with poached eggs

This punchy dish can be prepared in advance. Cook until the end of step 2, then gently reheat and crack in the eggs.

TAKES 1 HOUR 20 MINUTES • SERVES 4

1 tbsp olive oil
1 large onion, chopped
1 red or orange pepper, deseeded and thinly sliced
2 garlic cloves, finely chopped
1 tbsp chopped fresh rosemary
1 aubergine, diced
2 courgettes, diced
400g can chopped tomatoes
1 tsp balsamic vinegar
4 eggs
handful of fresh basil leaves, to garnish
crusty bread, to serve

1 Heat the oil in a large frying pan. Add the onion, pepper, garlic and rosemary, then cook for 5 minutes, stirring frequently, until the onion has softened. Add the aubergine and courgettes, then cook for 2 minutes more.
2 Add the tomatoes, then fill the can with water, swirl it around and tip into the pan. Bring to the boil, cover, then simmer for 40 minutes, uncovering after 20 minutes, until reduced and pulpy.
3 Stir the vinegar into the ratatouille, then make four spaces for the eggs. Crack an egg into each hole and season with black pepper. Cover, then cook for 2–5 minutes until the eggs are set as softly or firmly as you like. Scatter over the basil and serve with some crusty bread to mop up the juices.

PER SERVING 190 kcals, protein 12g, carbs 13g, fat 11g, sat fat 2g, fibre 5g, sugar 10g, salt 0.36g

Springtime pasta

Filled pasta such as tortellini freezes really well and only takes 1–2 minutes more to cook than it would unfrozen. Use all frozen veg, or vary the recipe by using asparagus or broccoli instead.

TAKES 10 MINUTES • SERVES 2

250g pack frozen ricotta and spinach tortellini
50g/2oz frozen peas
50g/2oz frozen broad beans
1 tbsp olive oil
zest 1 lemon
50g/2oz ricotta

1 Bring a pan of salted water to the boil. Tip in the pasta and cook for 3–4 minutes, then lift it out with a slotted spoon into a large bowl. Add the peas and broad beans to the pan, bring back to boil, then boil for 1 minute or until tender.
2 Drain well, then add to the pasta and toss through the olive oil and lemon zest. Place on plates, dollop over the ricotta and serve.

PER SERVING 472 kcals, protein 18g, carbs 62g, fat 19g, sat fat 8g, fibre 5g, sugar 5g, salt 1.34g

Springtime pasta

Easy ratatouille with poached eggs

Spring vegetable pilau

Use whichever vegetables are in season for this light and pretty dish. To make it richer, add 100g/3½oz feta when you stir in the dill.

TAKES 20 MINUTES • SERVES 4

1 tbsp olive oil
1 onion, chopped
300g/10oz basmati rice
700ml/1¼ pints vegetable stock
100g pack asparagus, cut into 2cm/¾in chunks
large handful of peas, fresh or frozen
large handful of broad beans, fresh or frozen
1 courgette, sliced
small bunch of dill, chopped

1 Heat the oil in a frying pan and cook the onion for 5 minutes until soft. Tip in the rice, pour over the stock and stir. Bring to the boil, then lower the heat to a simmer, cover and cook for 10 minutes or until the rice is almost tender.
2 Add the vegetables to the pan, cover and let them steam for 2 minutes. Take the pan off the heat and leave to stand, covered, for another 2 minutes to absorb any more liquid. Stir in the dill just before serving.

PER SERVING 317 kcals, protein 9g, carbs 66g, fat 4g, sat fat 1g, fibre 3g, added sugar none, salt 0.58g

Summer veg and tofu bowl

Steaming is a great way of cooking food with flavourings. The results are light and tasty, and retain all the freshness of the ingredients.

TAKES 25 MINUTES • SERVES 2

1–2 carrots, cut into sticks if large
1–2 turnips, cut into wedges
1 tbsp dry sherry
2 tbsp soy sauce
1 courgette, cut into 1cm/½in slices
4–6 short asparagus spears
3 fresh shiitake or open-cup mushrooms, each sliced in 4
25g/1oz butter
2 spring onions, shredded
100g/3½oz smoked tofu, cubed

1 Mix the carrot and turnip with the sherry and soy sauce in a shallow heatproof bowl that will fit inside a steamer basket. Leave to marinate for 10 minutes.
2 Bring a pan of water to the boil, fit the steamer basket, then place the bowl of carrot and turnip inside. Cover and steam for 4–5 minutes.
3 Add the courgette, asparagus and mushrooms, stirring to mix. Dot with the butter, sprinkle with the spring onions, cover and continue steaming for another 3 minutes.
4 Add the tofu and continue steaming for 2 minutes. Remove the bowl and mix everything together before serving.

PER SERVING 206 kcals, protein 8g, carbs 11g, fat 13g, sat fat 6.9g, fibre 4.4g, added sugar 0.3g, salt 3.01g

Summer veg and tofu bowl

Spring vegetable pilau

Quorn and cashew nut stir-fry

A Chinese stir-fry that's perfect for all the family. Get all the ingredients prepared first so you can toss them straight into the pan.

TAKES 15 MINUTES • SERVES 2 (EASILY DOUBLED)

50g/2oz cashew nuts
1 tbsp vegetable oil
200g/7oz Quorn pieces
85g/3oz small broccoli florets
85g/3oz small cauliflower florets
2 tbsp hoisin sauce
1 red or yellow pepper, deseeded and sliced

1 Tip the cashews into a wok or deep, non-stick frying pan and dry fry over a medium heat for a few minutes until toasted. Remove and set aside. Heat the oil in the wok, add the Quorn, broccoli and cauliflower and stir fry for 2 minutes.
2 Mix the hoisin sauce with 6 tablespoons boiling water, pour into the wok and add the sliced pepper. Toss for 3 minutes, or until the pepper is just tender. Add seasoning to taste and serve sprinkled with the cashews.

PER SERVING 363 kcals, protein 23g, carbs 19g, fat 22g, sat fat 2.6g, fibre 9g, added sugar 5g, salt 1.43g

Vietnamese veggie hotpot

Vietnamese food is known for its hot, sour, sweet and fresh herby flavours. You'll find all of them in this reviving bowlful to be enjoyed by itself or with rice.

TAKES 25 MINUTES • SERVES 4

2 tsp vegetable oil
thumb-sized knob of ginger, shredded
2 garlic cloves, chopped
½ large butternut squash, peeled and cut into chunks
2 tsp soy sauce
2 tsp light muscovado sugar
200ml/7fl oz vegetable stock
100g/3½oz green beans, trimmed and sliced
4 spring onions, sliced
chopped fresh coriander, to garnish

1 Heat the oil in a medium-sized lidded pan. Add the ginger and garlic, then stir-fry for about 5 minutes. Add the squash, soy sauce, sugar and stock. Cover, then simmer for 10 minutes.
2 Remove the lid, add the green beans, then cook for 3 minutes more until the squash and beans are tender. Stir the spring onions through at the last minute, then sprinkle with coriander.

PER SERVING 75 kcals, protein 2g, carbs 13g, fat 2g, sat fat none, fibre 3g, sugar 9g, salt 0.53g

Vietnamese veggie hotpot

Quorn and cashew nut stir-fry

Paneer in herby tomato sauce

Paneer is a low-fat cheese often described as Indian cottage cheese, but it's firmer and keeps its shape in cooking.

TAKES 25–35 MINUTES • SERVES 2

½ tsp cumin seeds
1 green chilli, deseeded and chopped
4cm/1½in knob fresh root ginger, peeled and chopped
150g carton Greek yogurt
1 tsp light muscovado sugar
½ tsp garam masala
2 tbsp chopped fresh coriander leaves and stems
juice ½ lime
3 tbsp tomato purée
250g/9oz frozen peas
227g pack paneer (Indian cheese), cut into 1cm/½in cubes
2–3 firm red tomatoes, cut into wedges
handful of roasted cashew nuts, chopped, to serve

1 Toast the cumin seeds in a pan to darken – about 30 seconds. Crush roughly with a rolling pin, then tip into a blender with the chilli, ginger, yogurt, sugar, garam masala, coriander, lime juice, tomato purée and 200ml/7fl oz water. Blitz until smooth.
2 Pour the sauce into the pan used to toast the cumin. Cook for 5 minutes, stirring often. Add the peas and simmer for 3–5 minutes until almost cooked.
3 Stir in the paneer and tomatoes, and heat through for 2–3 minutes. Scatter with cashew nuts just before serving.

PER SERVING 607 kcals, protein 44g, carbs 24g, fat 38g, sat fat 23g, fibre 8g, added sugar 3g, salt 3.26g

Mixed vegetable balti

Serve with warm mini naan breads. Alternatively, this curry mixture makes a great low-fat filling for baked potatoes.

TAKES 1¼–1½ HOURS • SERVES 4

1 tbsp vegetable oil
1 large onion, thickly sliced
1 large garlic clove, crushed
1 eating apple, peeled, cored and chopped into chunks
3 tbsp balti curry paste
1 medium butternut squash, peeled and cut into chunks
2 large carrots, thickly sliced
200g/7oz turnips, cut into chunks
1 cauliflower, about 500g/1lb 2oz, broken into florets
400g can chopped tomatoes
425ml/¾ pint vegetable stock
4 tbsp chopped coriander, plus extra to serve
150g carton low-fat natural yogurt

1 Heat the oil in a large pan and cook the onion, garlic and apple gently, stirring occasionally, until the onion softens – about 5–8 minutes. Stir in the curry paste.
2 Tip the fresh vegetables, tomatoes and stock into the pan. Stir in 3 tablespoons of the coriander. Bring to the boil, lower the heat, cover and cook for 30 minutes.
3 Remove the lid and cook for another 20 minutes until the vegetables are soft and the liquid has reduced a little. Season with salt and pepper.
4 Mix the remaining coriander into the yogurt to make a raita. Ladle the curry into bowls, drizzle over some raita and sprinkle with extra coriander. Serve with the remaining raita.

PER SERVING 201 kcals, protein 11g, carbs 25g, fat 7g, sat fat 1g, fibre 7g, added sugar none, salt 1.13g

Mixed vegetable balti

Paneer in herby tomato sauce

Spicy pea curry

This is a gently spiced and very tasty curry that suits all tastes. Peas are quick-frozen within a few hours of picking, so stay deliciously fresh.

TAKES 40–50 MINUTES • SERVES 4

2 tbsp vegetable oil
227g pack paneer (Indian cheese), torn into pieces
1 onion, thinly sliced
2 tbsp mild curry paste
450g/1lb potatoes, peeled and cut into chunks
400g can chopped tomatoes with garlic
300ml/½ pint vegetable stock
300g/10oz frozen peas
Indian bread, to serve

1 Heat 1 tablespoon of the oil in a large saucepan. Fry the paneer for 2–3 minutes, stirring, until crisp and golden. Remove with a slotted spoon and set aside.
2 Fry the onion in the remaining oil for 4–5 minutes until soft and just beginning to brown. Add the curry paste and fry, stirring, for 2 minutes.
3 Add the potatoes, tomatoes, stock and paneer, bring to the boil and simmer for 15 minutes. Add the peas, bring to the boil and simmer for 5 minutes longer. Season and serve with peshwari naan or other Indian bread.

PER SERVING 404 kcals, protein 20g, carbs 32g, fat 22g, sat fat 9g, fibre 7g, added sugar none, salt 2.84g

Curried rice with spinach

Warming and tasty, practically no preparation, superhealthy, uses storecupboard ingredients – one-pot dishes don't get better than this.

TAKES 20 MINUTES • SERVES 4

1 tbsp sunflower oil
2 garlic cloves, crushed
2 tbsp medium curry paste (Madras is a good one to use)
250g/9oz basmati rice, rinsed
450ml/16fl oz vegetable stock
400g can chickpeas, drained and rinsed
handful of raisins
175g/6oz frozen leaf spinach, thawed
handful of cashew nuts
natural yogurt, to serve (optional)

1 Heat the oil in a large, non-stick pan that has a lid, then fry the garlic and curry paste over a medium heat for 1 minute, until it smells toasty.
2 Tip the rice into the pan with the stock, chickpeas and raisins, and stir well with a fork to stop the rice from clumping. Season with salt and pepper, then cover and bring to the boil. Reduce to a medium heat and cook for 12–15 minutes or until all the liquid has been absorbed and the rice is tender.
3 Squeeze the excess water from the spinach with your hands. Tip it into the pan along with 2 tablespoons hot water, then fluff up the rice with a fork, making sure the spinach is mixed in well. Toss in the cashews. Serve drizzled with natural yogurt, if you like.

PER SERVING 380 kcals, protein 12g, carbs 66g, fat 9g, sat fat 1g, fibre 4g, added sugar none, salt 1.02g

Spicy pea curry

Curried rice with spinach

Thai red squash curry

You can vary the vegetables – try sweet potatoes, sugar snap peas and bamboo shoots – and scatter over cashew nuts.

TAKES 30 MINUTES • SERVES 4

1 small butternut squash, about 700g/1lb 9oz
200g pack mixed mangetout and baby corn
2 tbsp sunflower oil
1–2 tbsp Thai red curry paste, to taste
400ml can coconut milk
150ml/¼ pint vegetable stock
2 tbsp soy sauce
1 tbsp light muscovado sugar
juice ½ lime
naan bread or chapatis, to serve

1 Cut off the ends of the squash, quarter lengthways, then scoop out the fibres and seeds. Peel, then cut into chunks. Halve the baby corn lengthways.
2 Heat the oil in a saucepan and fry the paste gently for 1–2 minutes. Add the coconut milk, stock, soy sauce and sugar and bring to the boil.
3 Add the squash and baby corn, and salt to taste, cover and simmer for 10–12 minutes. Add the lime juice and mangetout, and simmer for 1 minute. Serve hot, with naan bread or chapatis.

PER SERVING 283 kcals, protein 4.4g, carbs 16.2g, fat 22.6g, sat fat 14.6g, fibre 2.2g, added sugar 5.3g, salt 1.95g

Singapore noodles with tofu

You'll love the combination of fresh tastes and textures in this dish – the crunch from the veg, the smooth noodles and the soft tofu, combined with a sweet and spicy sauce.

TAKES 25 MINUTES • SERVES 2 (EASILY DOUBLED)

140g/5oz firm tofu
2 tbsp sunflower oil
3 spring onions, shredded
1 small knob ginger, finely chopped
1 red pepper, deseeded and thinly sliced
100g/3½oz mangetout
300g pack straight-to-wok thin rice noodles
100g/3½oz beansprouts
1 tsp tikka masala curry paste
2 tsp reduced-salt soy sauce
1 tbsp sweet chilli sauce
roughly chopped fresh coriander and lime wedges, to garnish

1 Rinse the tofu in cold water, then cut into small chunks. Pat dry with kitchen paper. Heat 1 tablespoon of the oil in a wok or large frying pan, add the tofu, then stir-fry for 2–3 minutes until lightly browned. Drain on kitchen paper.
2 Add the remaining oil to the wok and let it heat up. Tip in the spring onions, ginger, pepper and mangetout, then stir-fry for 1 minute. Add the noodles and beansprouts, then stir to mix. Blend together the curry paste, soy, chilli sauce and 1 tablespoon water, then add to the wok, stirring until everything is well coated in the sauce. Serve sprinkled with coriander, with lime wedges for squeezing over on the side.

PER SERVING 392 kcals, protein 12g, carbs 57g, fat 15g, sat fat 2g, fibre 4g, sugar 12g, salt 3.20g

Thai red squash curry

Singapore noodles with tofu

Broccoli, walnut and blue cheese pasta

Add colour, crunch and a dollop of cheesy indulgence to your weeknight pasta with this simple recipe.

TAKES 15 MINUTES • SERVES 2

200g/7oz penne
250g/9oz broccoli florets
2 tbsp olive oil
4 tbsp walnut pieces
100g/3½oz creamy blue cheese, such as dolcelatte, cubed
squeeze of fresh lemon juice, to taste

1 Cook the pasta according to the packet instructions and then, 4 minutes before the end of cooking, throw in the broccoli. Drain, keeping a cup of the cooking water, then set aside.
2 Heat the oil in the pan, then add the walnuts and fry gently for 1 minute. Add 4 tablespoons of the reserved cooking water to the walnuts. Stir in the cheese until it melts, season, then stir in the lemon juice to taste. Tip the drained pasta and broccoli into the sauce, toss well, then serve.

PER SERVING 758 kcals, protein 28g, carbs 80g, fat 38g, sat fat 12g, fibre 7g, sugar 6g, salt 0.82g

Vegetable casserole with dumplings

The wine really adds flavour to this warming dish, and the baby vegetables look so pretty, too.

TAKES 1¾–2 HOURS • SERVES 6

8 shallots, halved lengthways
3 tbsp light olive oil
250g/9oz new potatoes, halved
1 chilli, deseeded and chopped
200g/7oz baby carrots, scraped
500g/1lb 2oz fennel, cut into wedges
300ml/½ pint fruity white wine
600ml/1 pint vegetable stock
200g/7oz green beans, halved
250g/9oz mushrooms,halved
200g/7oz baby courgettes, chopped
1 tbsp each snipped chives and parsley
FOR THE DUMPLINGS
50g/2oz butter, cut into pieces
100g/3½oz self-raising flour
50g/2oz mature Cheddar, grated
3 tbsp finely chopped fresh parsley

1 Fry the shallots in the oil in a flameproof casserole until softened. Add the potatoes and fry for 5–7 minutes, then add the chilli, carrots and fennel and fry until coloured. Pour in the wine and stock and bring to the boil. Season, cover and simmer for 10 minutes.
2 Make the dumplings. Rub the butter into the flour, stir in the cheese, parsley and seasoning, then stir in about 2 tablespoons water to form a soft dough. Break off small pieces and form into 20–25 dumplings.
3 Add the beans to the pan and simmer for 5 minutes, then add the mushrooms and courgettes. Bring to the boil and stir well. Place the dumplings on top. Cover and simmer for 15 minutes until the dumplings have risen. Taste for seasoning and serve sprinkled with the chives and parsley.

PER SERVING 285 kcals, protein 8g, carbs 28g, fat 17g, sat fat 7g, fibre 5.6g, added sugar none, salt 0.85g

Broccoli, walnut and blue cheese pasta

Vegetable casserole with dumplings

More-ish mushrooms and rice

Take handful of simple storecupboard ingredients and turn them into this hearty, comforting family supper.

TAKES 50 MINUTES • SERVES 4

200g/7oz basmati rice
1 tbsp olive oil
1 large onion, chopped
2 tsp chopped fresh rosemary or 1 tsp dried
250g/9oz chestnut mushrooms, quartered
2 red peppers, deseeded and sliced
400g can chopped tomatoes
425ml/¾ pint vegetable stock
chopped fresh parsley, to garnish

1 Heat the oven to 190C/170C fan/gas 5. Tip the rice into a sieve, rinse under cold running water, then leave to drain. Heat the oil in a flameproof casserole, add the onion, then fry until softened, which will take around 5 minutes.
2 Stir in the rosemary and mushrooms, then fry briefly. Add the rice, stir to coat in the oil, then tip in the peppers, tomatoes, stock and seasoning. Bring to the boil, stir, cover tightly with a lid, then bake for 20–25 minutes until the rice is tender. Scatter over the parsley and serve.

PER SERVING 282 kcals, protein 9g, carbs 55g, fat 5g, sat fat 1g, fibre 4g, sugar 7g, salt 0.36g

Roasted vegetables with cheese

A colourful and hearty supper dish for autumn.

TAKES 40–50 MINUTES • SERVES 2

1 red onion
1 large butternut squash (about 600–700g/1lb 5oz–1lb 9oz) peeled, deseeded and cut into large bite-size pieces
6 tbsp olive oil
2 tbsp chopped fresh sage leaves
1 large courgette, thickly sliced
1 tbsp balsamic or sherry vinegar
100g/3½oz Lancashire cheese

1 Heat the oven to 200C/180C fan/gas 6. Halve the onion lengthways and trim the root end, leaving a little root left on to hold the segments together. Peel each half and cut into 4 wedges. Scatter the onion and squash in a large roasting tin so they have plenty of room, and toss with 5 tablespoons of the oil, the sage and seasoning to taste. Roast for 20 minutes, stirring halfway.
2 Toss the courgette slices with the remaining oil. Remove the tin from the oven and push the squash and onion to one side. Lay the courgette slices flat on the base of the tin, season and roast for 10 minutes, until all the vegetables are tender.
3 Sprinkle the vinegar over the vegetables and toss to mix, then crumble over the cheese and toss lightly so the cheese melts a little. Serve.

PER SERVING 306 kcals, protein 8g, carbs 14g, fat 25g, sat fat 7g, fibre 3g, added sugar none, salt 0.39g

Roasted vegetables with cheese

More-ish mushrooms and rice

Tomato baked eggs

This is such a simple recipe and is welcome at any time of day – for a weekend lunch, an easy supper or even a leisurely breakfast.

TAKES ABOUT 1 HOUR • SERVES 4

900g/2lb ripe vine tomatoes
3 garlic cloves, thinly sliced
3 tbsp olive oil
4 free-range eggs
2 tbsp chopped parsley and/or chives
toast or ciabatta and green salad, to serve

1 Heat the oven to 200C/180C fan/gas 6. Cut the tomatoes into quarters or thick wedges, depending on their size, then spread them over the base of a fairly shallow, large ovenproof dish. Sprinkle the garlic over the tomatoes, drizzle with the oil and season well. Stir until the tomatoes are glistening, then bake for 40 minutes until softened and tinged with brown.
2 Make four gaps among the tomatoes, break an egg into each gap and cover the dish with foil. Return the dish to the oven for 5–10 minutes until the eggs are set to your liking. Scatter over the herbs and serve piping hot, with thick slices of toast or warm ciabatta and a green salad on the side.

PER SERVING 204 kcals, protein 9g, carbs 7g, fat 16g, sat fat 3g, fibre 3g, added sugar none, salt 0.27g

Oven egg and chips

Want to be practical but need some inspiration? This dish is a great way of using up potatoes and it's not as unhealthy as it looks.

TAKES 50–60 MINUTES • SERVES 2

450g/1lb floury potatoes, such as King Edward
   or Maris Piper
2 garlic cloves, sliced
4 fresh rosemary sprigs or 1 tsp dried
2 tbsp olive oil
2 eggs

1 Heat the oven to 220C/200C fan/gas 7. Without peeling, cut the potatoes into thick chips. Tip them into a roasting pan (non-stick is best) and scatter over the garlic. Strip the rosemary leaves from the sprigs and sprinkle them, or the dried rosemary, over too. Drizzle with the oil, season well, then toss the chips to coat them in oil and flavourings.
2 Oven-roast the chips for 35–40 minutes until just cooked and golden, shaking the tin halfway through.
3 Make two gaps in the chips and break an egg into each gap. Return to the oven for 3–5 minutes until the eggs are cooked to your liking.

PER SERVING 348 kcals, protein 11g, carbs 40g, fat 17g, sat fat 3g, fibre 3g, added sugar none, salt 0.22g

Tomato baked eggs

Oven egg and chips

Superhealthy pizza

Making pizza dough from scratch is so much easier than you might think and takes just minutes in the food processor.

TAKES 20 MINUTES • SERVES 2

100g/3½oz each strong white and strong
   wholewheat flour
7g sachet easy-blend dried yeast
125ml/4fl oz warm water
FOR THE TOPPING
200g can chopped tomatoes, juice drained
handful of cherry tomatoes, halved
1 large courgette, thinly sliced using a peeler
25g/1oz mozzarella, torn into pieces
1 tsp capers in brine, drained
8 green olives, roughly chopped
1 garlic clove, finely chopped
1 tbsp olive oil
2 tbsp chopped fresh parsley, to garnish

1 Mix the flours and yeast with a pinch of salt in a food processor fitted with a dough blade. Pour in the water and mix to a soft dough, then work for 1 minute. Remove the dough and roll out on a lightly floured surface to a round about 30cm across. Lift on to an oiled baking sheet.
2 Spread the canned tomatoes over the dough to within 2cm of the edge. Arrange the cherry tomatoes and courgette slices over the top, then scatter with the mozzarella. Mix together the capers, olives and garlic, then scatter over the top. Drizzle evenly with the oil. Leave to rise for 20 minutes. Heat the oven to 240C/220C fan/gas 9.
3 Bake the pizza for 10–12 minutes until crisp and golden around the edge. Scatter with the parsley to serve.

PER SERVING 479 kcals, protein 19g, carbs 78g, fat 13g, sat fat 3g, fibre 10g, sugar 9g, salt 1.43g

Risotto with squash and sage

Our butternut risotto is so satisfying – bags of flavour, two of your 5-a-day and just one pan to deal with.

TAKES 1 HOUR • SERVES 4

2½ tbsp olive oil
handful of fresh sage leaves, 6 finely chopped,
   the rest left whole
4 slices dried porcini mushrooms
2 litres/3½ pints hot low-salt vegetable stock
1 onion, finely chopped
2 garlic cloves, finely chopped
2 fresh thyme sprigs
700g/1lb 9oz butternut squash, peeled and
   cubed
350g/12oz carnaroli (or arborio) rice
100ml/3½fl oz dry white wine
handful of flat-leaf parsley, chopped
50g/2oz Parmesan, grated
2 tbsp light mascarpone

1 Heat ½ tablespoon oil in a pan, fry the whole sage leaves for a few seconds until starting to colour. Drain on kitchen paper. Soak the mushrooms in the hot stock.
2 Heat 2 tablespoons oil in the cooled pan. Add the onion, garlic, chopped sage, thyme and squash; gently fry for 10 minutes. On a medium heat, tip in the rice. Stir for 3 minutes then add the wine and stir for 1 minute.
3 Stir in a ladleful of hot stock (leaving the porcini behind). Continue gradually adding and stirring until the rice is soft with a little bite and almost all the stock is used. Season.
4 Off the heat, add a splash more stock to the pan then scatter over the parsley, half the Parmesan and the mascarpone. Cover for 3–4 minutes then stir. Scatter with remaining Parmesan and the crisp sage leaves to serve.

PER SERVING 517 kcals, protein 15g, carbs 85g, fat 15g, sat fat 5g, fibre 5g, sugar 10g, salt 0.37g

Superhealthy pizza

Risotto with squash and sage

Bean and vegetable chilli

Sweet red pepper sauce makes an interesting change from tomato sauce. Serve this veggie chilli with garlic bread and a salad.

TAKES 40–50 MINUTES • SERVES 4

3 tbsp olive oil
2 onions, chopped
2 tsp caster sugar
250g/9oz chestnut mushrooms, sliced
2 garlic cloves, sliced
2 tsp mild chilli powder
1 tbsp ground coriander
290–350g jar sweet red pepper sauce
300ml/½ pint vegetable stock
410g can chickpeas, drained and rinsed
410g can black-eye beans, drained and rinsed
garlic bread and mixed salad, to serve

1 Heat the oil in a large, heavy-based saucepan and fry the onions and sugar over a high heat until deep golden. Add the mushrooms, garlic, chilli powder and ground coriander and fry for 2–3 minutes.

2 Stir in the pepper sauce, stock, chickpeas and beans and bring to the boil. Reduce the heat, cover and simmer gently for 20 minutes. Season and serve, with garlic bread and a mixed salad.

PER SERVING 303 kcals, protein 14g, carbs 36g, fat 13g, sat fat 2g, fibre 8g, added sugar 5g, salt 1.4g

Macaroni cheese with mushrooms

Lighter than the original, this basic pasta dish is one to experiment with.

TAKES 20–25 MINUTES • SERVES 2

200g/7oz macaroni
2 leeks
6 mushrooms
4 tomatoes
2 tbsp olive oil
2 x mini garlic and herb soft cheeses, or mini Bries or blue cheeses

1 Fill a large sauté pan with boiling water. Tip in the macaroni and cook according to the pack instructions until tender. (It may take slightly longer than suggested.) Meanwhile, trim, slice and wash the leeks, quarter the mushrooms and roughly chop the tomatoes.

2 Drain the pasta and keep warm. Heat the oil in the pan, add the leeks and mushrooms and fry for 4–6 minutes until the leeks are tender. Toss in the tomatoes at the last minute. Season with salt if you want to, and black pepper. Stir in the macaroni and warm through, then crumble the cheese over and let it melt slightly before serving.

PER SERVING 619 kcals, protein 17g, carbs 85g, fat 26g, sat fat 10g, fibre 8g, added sugar none, salt 0.3g

Roast summer vegetables and chickpeas

Summery tomato-based stews like this one are perfect to make ahead. You could switch the chickpeas for butter or cannellini beans.

TAKES 1 HOUR 10 MINUTES • SERVES 4

3 courgettes, thickly sliced
1 aubergine, cut into thick fingers
3 garlic cloves, chopped
2 red peppers, deseeded and chopped into chunks
2 large baking potatoes, peeled and cut into bite-size chunks
1 onion, chopped
1 tbsp coriander seeds
4 tbsp olive oil
400g can chopped tomatoes
400g can chickpeas, drained and rinsed
small bunch of coriander, roughly chopped
hunks of bread, to serve

1 Heat the oven to 220C/200C fan/gas 7. Tip all the vegetables into a large roasting tin or flameproof dish and toss with the coriander seeds, most of the olive oil and some salt and pepper. Spread everything out in a single layer and roast for 45 minutes, tossing once or twice until the vegetables are roasted and brown round the edges.
2 Place the tin over a low heat and add the tomatoes and chickpeas. Bring to a simmer and stir gently. Season to taste, drizzle with the remaining olive oil and scatter over the coriander. Serve from the tin or pile into a serving dish. Eat with hunks of bread.

PER SERVING 327 kcals, protein 11g, carbs 40g, fat 15g, sat fat 2g, fibre 9g, sugar 13g, salt 0.51g

Cheesy vegetable hotpot

This is vegetarian food at its easiest and most comforting.

TAKES 35–40 MINUTES • SERVES 4

3 leeks, trimmed, roughly sliced
large knob of butter
½ small Savoy cabbage, shredded
8 chestnut mushrooms, sliced
4 tbsp crème fraîche
3 medium potatoes, peeled and thinly sliced
1 small Camembert or other rinded soft cheese, sliced with the rind on
1 tbsp fresh thyme leaves

1 In a shallow microwavable dish, toss the leeks in half the butter and microwave on High for 5 minutes until they begin to soften. Stir in the cabbage and mushrooms and add the crème fraîche. Lay the potato slices over the vegetables, pressing them down with a fish slice.
2 Dot the potatoes with the remaining butter and microwave, uncovered, for 15–20 minutes on High until they are done. Scatter over the cheese and thyme, and either microwave on High to melt for 2 minutes, or grill until crisp and brown. Leave to stand for a few minutes before serving.

PER SERVING 308 kcals, protein 15g, carbs 19g, fat 20g, sat fat 12g, fibre 5g, added sugar none, salt 0.83g

Chunky chilli wraps, page 162

Feeding a crowd

Warm duck salad with walnut and orange dressing

Try this for a stress-free lunch that's sure to impress.

TAKES 35 MINUTES • SERVES 4

4 duck breasts
4 medium potatoes, peeled and diced
16 walnut halves
250g pack vacuum-packed cooked beetroot (without vinegar), cut into wedges
100g bag watercress, large stems removed
4 spring onions, thinly sliced
1 chicory head, separated into leaves and the core sliced
3 small oranges, peeled and sliced
FOR THE DRESSING
4 tbsp walnut oil
4 tsp red wine vinegar
1 tbsp chunky marmalade

1 Mix together all the dressing ingredients, season, then set aside.
2 Heat a roasting pan on the hob, add the duck, skin-side down, then gently fry for around 10 minutes. Turn the duck over for a second to seal, then remove.
3 Heat the oven to 220C/200C fan/gas 7. Toss the potatoes in the duck fat and fry until golden. Lift out of the fat with a slotted spoon and discard the fat. Put the potatoes, nuts and beetroot back into the pan. Put the duck on a roasting rack above the veg. Roast for 15 minutes.
4 Toss together the watercress, spring onions, chicory and oranges with most of the dressing. Pile on to plates with the beetroot, potatoes and walnuts. Slice the duck, arrange on top of the salad and drizzle with the remaining dressing. Serve warm.

PER SERVING 742 kcals, protein 34g, carbs 40g, fat 51g, sat fat 10g, fibre 6g, sugar 18g, salt 0.54g

Italian chicken with ham, basil and beans

Fresh tomatoes and garlic cook down to sweet, saucy pan juices in this sophisticated but so easy recipe.

TAKES ABOUT 1½ HOURS • SERVES 4

8 skinless chicken thighs, bone in
1 large bunch fresh basil
8 slices prosciutto or other dry-cured ham
2 tbsp olive oil
2 garlic bulbs, halved across the middle
800g/1lb 12oz mix yellow and red tomatoes, halved or quartered if large
175ml/6fl oz dry white wine
400g can cannellini or other white beans, drained and rinsed

1 Season the chicken thighs. Pinch off eight basil sprigs and lay one on top of each chicken thigh. Wrap each thigh in a piece of ham, with the ends tucked underneath.
2 Heat the oven to 160C/140C fan/gas 3. Heat the oil over a medium heat in a large roasting tin. Add the chicken and fry for 4 minutes each side or until the ham is just crisped and the chicken lightly golden.
3 Add the tomatoes, garlic, half the remaining basil leaves and the wine. Season, cover with foil, then cook in the oven for 40 minutes.
4 Take out of the oven; turn the temperature up to 220C/200C fan/gas 7. Remove the foil then stir the beans into the tomatoey juices. Return to the oven, uncovered, and cook for 30 minutes until the tomatoes, chicken and garlic are starting to crisp and chicken is very tender. Scatter over the remaining basil.

PER SERVING 455 kcals, protein 55g, carbs 22g, fat 16g, sat fat 4g, fibre 6g, sugar 10g, salt 1.79g

Warm duck salad with walnut and orange dressing

Italian chicken with ham, basil and beans

Sirloin steaks with pizzaiola sauce

This simple recipe is ideal for a special mid-week supper, as it can be cooked very quickly when you get home from work. Any leftover sauce is stunning saved and used on pizzas or folded through pasta.

TAKES 30 MINUTES • SERVES 4

50ml/2fl oz olive oil
1 garlic clove, roughly chopped
4 sirloin steaks, each about 140g/5oz
2 x 400g cans chopped tomatoes
2 tsp dried oregano
bread or new potatoes, to serve
rocket leaves, to garnish

1 Heat a heavy-based frying pan over a high heat, then add the olive oil and garlic. Season the meat and then, two at a time, quickly brown the steaks in the pan on both sides.
2 Put all four steaks in the pan, add the tomatoes, season with salt and pepper, then turn down the heat. Sprinkle the oregano over the meat and tomatoes, partially cover the pan, then simmer gently for 10 minutes.
3 Lift the tender pieces of meat from the pan, cover with foil, then set aside. Increase the heat, then simmer the tomato sauce for about 10 minutes, until it has reduced by half. Spoon the sauce over the steak and serve with bread or new potatoes and a garnish of rocket leaves.

PER SERVING 415 kcals, protein 33g, carbs 5g, fat 29g, sat fat 10g, fibre 2g, sugar 4g, salt 0.63g

Marmite carbonade

Our big beef casserole is all the beefier for its crisp Marmite toasts. Like any stew, it's even better left to cool and then chill overnight, which also spreads the workload.

TAKES 2 HOURS 50 MINUTES • SERVES 8

85g/3oz unsalted butter, plus extra for spreading
4 onions, halved and sliced
3 garlic cloves, peeled and smashed
1.5kg/3lb 5oz stewing steak, cut into large cubes
850ml/1½ pints beef stock
1½ tbsp plain flour
400ml can stout
about 10 fresh thyme sprigs, tied into bunch
2 bay leaves
1 tbsp light muscovado sugar
2 tsp red wine vinegar
2–4 tbsp mushroom ketchup
1 celery heart, trimmed and sliced
about 2 tsp Marmite
about ¾ baguette, cut into 25 or so thin slices

1 Heat the oven to 180C/160C fan/gas 4. Melt half the butter in a casserole. Gently fry the onions for 8–12 minutes; add the garlic for 1 minute then tip into a bowl. Increase the heat, and brown the beef in batches, adding butter each time. Deglaze the pan as you go: splash a little stock into the pan, stir, then tip into a bowl.
2 Return the onions and beef to the pan, stir in the flour, then pour over stout, stock and deglazing liquid. Add the herbs, sugar, vinegar and mushroom ketchup. Season, bring to the boil, cover, then cook in the oven for 1½ hours. Skim off any fat.
3 Turn the oven up to 200C/180C fan/gas 6. Discard the herbs, then add the celery. Mix the remaining butter with the Marmite, then spread over the bread. Place on top of the stew and cook for 30–40 minutes.

PER SERVING 520 kcals, protein 44g, carbs 24g, fat 27g, sat fat 13g, fibre 2g, sugar 7g, salt 1.3g

Marmite carbonade

Sirloin steaks with pizzaiola sauce

Roast chicken with butternut squash, chorizo and chilli

Swap the usual spuds and gravy for warmly spiced veg and tasty nuggets of chorizo in this aromatic autumnal roast.

TAKES 2½ HOURS • SERVES 6

4 medium red onions, 1 halved, the rest cut into wedges
12 fresh sage leaves, 8 shredded,
    4 left whole, plus more to garnish
1 large whole chicken, about 2.25kg/5lb
1 tbsp olive oil, plus extra for greasing
1 butternut squash, peeled and cut into large chunky wedges
500g pack Charlotte potatoes, halved
2 red chillies, seeds left in and sliced
110g pack chorizo sausage, sliced
1 garlic bulb, separated into cloves

1 Heat the oven to 190C/170C fan/gas 5. Tuck two onion halves and four sage leaves inside the chicken cavity, rub the skin with a little oil, then season. Cook in the oven in a large roasting tin, breast-side down for 45 minutes. Turn over then roast for around 30 minutes more.
2 Toss the onion wedges with the shredded sage, squash, potatoes, chillies, chorizo, garlic cloves, 1 tablespoon oil and seasoning. Scatter round the chicken, toss in the pan juices; roast for 45 minutes.
3 Set the chicken aside to rest, turn the oven up to 220C/200C fan/gas 7. Toss the vegetables in the pan juices, spread over the tin to give them a bit of space, then return to the oven for 15 minutes to brown. Garnish the chicken with fresh sage leaves and serve.

PER SERVING 501 kcals, protein 42g, carbs 30g, fat 25g, sat fat 8g, fibre 4g, sugar 11g, salt 0.57g

Herby baked lamb in tomato sauce

This is so easy to prepare and the dish almost looks after itself – the end result is packed with flavour.

TAKES 4¼ HOURS • SERVES 4 (WITH LEFTOVERS)

1.8kg/4lb–2kg/4lb 8oz shoulder of lamb
2 tbsp olive oil
3 fresh oregano sprigs, leaves stripped from 2
3 fresh rosemary sprigs, leaves stripped from 2
3 garlic cloves, roughly chopped
600ml/1 pint red wine
2 x 400g cans chopped tomatoes
1 tbsp caster sugar

1 Heat the oven to 220C/200C fan/gas 7. Put the lamb into a large ovenproof dish. Whizz the oil, oregano, rosemary leaves, garlic and seasoning in a food processor. Rub all over the lamb; roast for 20 minutes. Cover, lower the oven to 150C/130C fan/gas 2, then roast for 3 hours more.
2 Remove from the oven, spoon off the fat, leaving any meat juices in the pan. Add the wine, tomatoes and remaining herb sprigs, then return to the oven, uncovered, for 40 minutes more. The lamb should now be meltingly tender. Carefully transfer the lamb to a plate; cover and leave to rest.
3 Meanwhile, simmer the sauce for about 10–15 minutes until thickened. Season with the sugar, and a little salt and pepper, then return the lamb to the pan to serve.

PER SERVING 595 kcals, protein 42g, carbs 11g, fat 40g, sat fat 19g, fibre 1g, sugar 10g, salt 0.51g

Roast chicken with butternut squash, chorizo and chilli

Herby baked lamb in tomato sauce

Feta-crusted lamb with rich tomato sauce

If you want to cook this irresistibly easy lamb for four, simply double the ingredients and make sure you use a large-enough pan.

TAKES 50 MINUTES, PLUS MARINATING AND RESTING • SERVES 2

7- or 8-bone rack of lamb, trimmed of fat, then cut into two racks
2 tbsp extra-virgin olive oil, plus extra to drizzle
a few fresh thyme sprigs, left whole, plus extra to serve
4 garlic cloves, crushed
zest 1 lemon
1 tsp dried oregano, plus a pinch
20g pack flat-leaf parsley, stalks finely chopped, leaves roughly
400g can cherry tomatoes
50g/2oz feta, finely crumbled
½ slice white bread (day old if you can), whizzed into crumbs

1 Put the racks into a food bag along with 1 tablespoon oil, the thyme sprigs, half the garlic, zest and oregano. Chill for 30 minutes or up to 24 hours. Make sure the lamb has returned to room temperature before cooking.
2 Heat a casserole dish; add 1 tablespoon oil. Add the remaining garlic and the parsley stalks; soften for 1 minute. Add the tomatoes and pinch of oregano; simmer for 5 minutes. Add half the parsley leaves. Heat the oven to 230C/210C fan/gas 8. Meanwhile, mix the remaining parsley, zest and oregano, plus the feta and crumbs to make a crust.
3 Season the meat, then press the crust on. Sit the racks in the sauce, crust-side up. Strew the extra thyme sprigs over, then drizzle with oil. Roast uncovered for 20 minutes until golden and the sauce thickened. Rest for 10 minutes, then serve.

PER SERVING 582 kcals, protein 26g, carbs 12g, fat 48g, sat fat 18g, fibre 3g, sugar 6g, salt 1.47g

Whole roast bream with potatoes and olives

Don't be daunted by cooking whole fish – this special main course is easy to make and sure to impress.

TAKES 50 MINUTES • SERVES 2 (EASILY DOUBLED)

400g/14oz new or small potatoes, thickly sliced
2 tbsp olive oil
large handful of pitted small black olives
1 garlic clove, chopped
1 large bunch flat-leaf parsley, leaves roughly chopped, stalks reserved
zest ½ lemon
1 whole sea bream, about 450g/1lb, gutted, head on (ask your fishmonger to do this for you)
1 small glass white wine

1 Heat the oven to 220C/200C fan/gas 7. Put the potatoes in a gratin dish, toss with 1 tablespoon oil then roast for 20 minutes until just starting to soften. Toss the olives, garlic, half the chopped parsley, the lemon zest and some salt and pepper with the potatoes then spread over the dish.
2 Season the fish and place the parsley stalks in the cavity. Lay the fish on top of the potatoes and drizzle with the rest of the olive oil. Bake for 15 minutes. Pour the wine over, then return to the oven for 10 minutes more until the potatoes have browned and the fish is cooked.
3 Remove the dish from the oven, scatter over the rest of the parsley and bring the dish to the table. When you serve up, don't forget the lovely white wine juices in the bottom of the dish.

PER SERVING 463 kcals, protein 34g, carbs 36g, fat 20g, sat fat 3g, fibre 3g, sugar 6g, salt 0.81g

Feta-crusted lamb with rich tomato sauce

Whole roast bream with potatoes and olives

Chicken with spring vegetables

Play around with this recipe, you could try broccoli sprigs and green beans instead.

TAKES 1¼–1½ HOURS • SERVES 8

2 tbsp olive oil
25g/1oz butter
8 large boneless, skinless chicken breasts, each cut into 3 pieces
8 shallots, halved
2 garlic cloves, roughly chopped
450g/1lb baby new potatoes, halved
450g/1lb baby carrots, scrubbed
3 tbsp plain flour
1½ tbsp Dijon mustard
425ml/¾ pint dry white wine
425ml/¾ pint chicken stock
225g/8oz asparagus tips, trimmed
225g/8oz shelled broad beans, thawed if frozen
1 tbsp lemon juice
100ml/3½fl oz double cream
handful of chopped mixed fresh parsley and tarragon
crusty bread, to serve

1 Heat the oil and butter in a large sauté pan and cook the chicken in batches for 3–4 minutes until golden all over. Remove from the pan and set aside. Add the shallots, garlic, potatoes and carrots to the pan and toss together. Cook for about 5 minutes until beginning to turn golden. Sprinkle over the flour, stir in the mustard and toss well, then pour over the white wine and gently simmer until reduced by about half.
2 Pour in the stock, bring to a simmer, then return the chicken to the pan. Cover and simmer for about 15 minutes.
3 Scatter over the asparagus and broad beans, without stirring, cover and simmer for 8 minutes. Stir in the lemon juice, cream, parsley and tarragon and heat through. Serve with crusty bread.

PER SERVING 414 kcals, protein 42g, carbs 23g, fat 14g, sat fat 6g, fibre 5g, added sugar none, salt 0.92g

Hob-to-table moussaka

This is a quick variation of the classic Greek dish. For an authentic Mediterranean meal, serve with toasted pitta bread.

TAKES 40–50 MINUTES • SERVES 8

2 tbsp olive oil
2 large onions, finely chopped
2 garlic cloves, finely chopped
1kg/2lb 4oz minced lamb
2 x 400g cans chopped tomatoes
3 tbsp tomato purée
2 tsp ground cinnamon
200g jar chargrilled aubergines in olive oil, drained and chopped
300g/10oz feta, crumbled
large handful of mint, chopped
green salad and toasted pitta bread, to serve

1 Heat the oil in a large deep frying pan or sauté pan. Toss in the onions and garlic and fry until soft. Add the mince and stir fry for about 10 minutes until browned.
2 Tip the tomatoes into the pan, add a canful of water and stir in the tomato purée and cinnamon. Season generously with salt and pepper. Leave the mince to simmer for 30 minutes, adding the aubergines halfway through.
3 Sprinkle the crumbled feta and chopped mint over the mince. Bring the moussaka to the table as the feta melts, and serve with a crunchy green salad and toasted pitta.

PER SERVING 454 kcals, protein 32g, carbs 10g, fat 32g, sat fat 14.1g, fibre 2.3g, added sugar none, salt 1.83g

Chicken with spring vegetables

Hob-to-table moussaka

Chunky chilli wraps

Once you're prepped, this dish only takes about 10 minutes to cook, so it's perfect for casual last-minute entertaining. Serve with a salad, if you like.

TAKES 35–45 MINUTES • SERVES 6

1 tbsp vegetable oil, plus a few extra drizzles
750g/1lb 10oz rump steak, sliced into
    thin strips
1 red onion, roughly chopped
4 mild green chillies, deseeded and chopped
1 tsp cumin seeds
1 tsp cayenne or hot chilli powder
400g can chopped tomatoes
420g can red kidney beans, drained and rinsed
200g/7oz roasted peppers from a jar, cut
    into strips
1 tsp Worcestershire sauce
TO SERVE
12 flour tortillas, warmed
284ml pot soured cream
handful of fresh mint, roughly chopped

1 Heat the oil in a wok until hot. Tip in a third of the beef and stir-fry for 2–3 minutes until it begins to brown. Scoop out the beef and put it on a plate. Repeat with the remaining beef, adding a drizzle more oil to the pan each time.
2 Toss the onion, chillies, cumin seeds and cayenne or chilli powder into the pan, stir and sizzle for 2 minutes. Lower the heat, tip in the tomatoes, kidney beans and roasted peppers. Return the beef to the pan and cook for 2 minutes, stirring occasionally, until bubbling. Add the Worcestershire sauce and continue to simmer gently for a further 2 minutes. Season to taste.
3 To serve, heat the tortillas according to the packet instructions. Pass round the warm tortillas for wrapping up the chilli, and bowls of soured cream and mint for drizzling and scattering over.

PER SERVING 644 kcals, protein 38g, carbs 54g, fat 32g, sat fat 13g, fibre 6g, added sugar none, salt 2.89g

Saucy summer lamb

Jars of artichokes in oil are a great storecupboard standby. They work beautifully with the mint and tomato in this lamb medley.

TAKES 1¼–1½ HOURS • SERVES 8

1kg/2lb 4oz ripe tomatoes
1.25kg/2lb 4oz cubed lamb (boneless neck,
    shoulder or leg)
3 tbsp olive oil
1 large Spanish onion, thinly sliced
290g jar artichoke hearts in oil, drained
large handful of mint leaves, roughly chopped

1 Make a cross in the bottom of each tomato with a sharp knife, then put a third of the tomatoes in a large bowl and cover with boiling water. Leave for a few minutes until the skins split, then drain and peel. Repeat with the remaining tomatoes, then chop them roughly.
2 Season the lamb. Heat 2 tablespoons of the oil in a large saucepan over a medium-high heat and fry the lamb in batches until browned. Put to one side. Lower the heat, add the remaining oil and the onion to the pan and fry for about 5 minutes until softened.
3 Return the lamb to the pan and stir in the tomatoes. Bring to the boil, lower the heat and splash in some hot water to cover the meat. Put the lid on and simmer for 50–60 minutes or until the lamb is tender. Stir in the artichokes and mint, heat through and season to taste.

PER SERVING 405 kcals, protein 31g, carbs 7g, fat 28g, sat fat 10.7g, fibre 2.3g, added sugar none, salt 0.68g

All-in-one leek and pork pot roast

Leeks are at their loveliest when slow cooked – they virtually melt into this stunning pot roast, perfect for friends to share.

TAKES 2¼ HOURS • SERVES 6

1kg/2lb 4oz boned and rolled shoulder pork
6 bay leaves
2 garlic cloves, sliced
1 bunch fresh thyme sprigs
25g/1oz butter
1 tbsp sunflower oil
2 onions, peeled and cut into wedges
5 juniper berries, crushed
1 tsp golden caster sugar
1 tbsp white wine vinegar
4 whole leeks, trimmed then each cut into 3
250ml/9fl oz white wine

1 Heat the oven to 180C/160C fan/gas 4. Untie and unroll the joint then lay four bay leaves, the sliced garlic and half the thyme sprigs along the centre of the meat. Retie with string.
2 Heat the butter and the oil in a casserole, then brown the pork on all sides; about 10 minutes. Add the onions, then cook for 5 minutes. Add the juniper berries, sugar and vinegar. Simmer, then tuck the leeks, remaining bay and thyme around the pork. Add the wine, cover, then cook in the oven for 1½–1¾ hours until the meat is tender.
3 To serve, remove the meat to a board. Season the veg, then use a slotted spoon to lift it into a bowl. Serve generous slices of meat with the bowl of vegetables and the sauce on the side.

PER SERVING 470 kcals, protein 32g, carbs 9g, fat 33g, sat fat 13g, fibre 3g, sugar 7g, salt 0.36g

Spicy lamb with chickpeas

Good-quality canned tomatoes really make a difference to the flavour of this dish.

TAKES 1½–1¾ HOURS • SERVES 8

1.25kg/2lb 8oz boneless lamb fillet or leg, cubed
2 x 400g cans tomatoes in rich juice
1 tbsp harissa paste, or to taste
2 x 410g cans chickpeas, drained and rinsed
large handful of coriander leaves, roughly
    chopped

1 Put the lamb and tomatoes in a large pan. Fill one of the tomato cans with water, pour into the pan and stir in the harissa with a good sprinkling of salt and pepper. Bring to the boil, then reduce the heat and cover the pan. Simmer gently, stirring occasionally, for 1¼–1½ hours or until the lamb is tender.
2 Tip in the chickpeas, stir well and heat through for 5 minutes. Taste for seasoning, adding more harissa, if you like. Serve scattered with coriander.

PER SERVING 406 kcals, protein 36g, carbs 13g, fat 24g, sat fat 10.8g, fibre 3.5g, added sugar none, salt 0.82g

Steak and mushroom goulash

For a vegetarian crowd, swap the meat for two 400g cans of chickpeas (drained and rinsed), and increase the mushrooms to 400g/14oz.

TAKES 50–60 MINUTES • SERVES 8

750g/1lb 10oz rump or sirloin steak, trimmed and cut into thin strips against the grain
3 tbsp vegetable oil
200g/7oz chestnut mushrooms, quartered
1 tbsp paprika
900g/2lb potatoes, peeled and cut into small chunks
500g jar passata (sieved tomatoes)
about 850ml/1½ pints beef stock
150g carton natural yogurt
handful of parsley leaves, roughly chopped

1 Season the steak well. Heat 1 tablespoon of the oil in a large flameproof casserole over a medium-high heat. Add about a third of the steak and fry for 2–3 minutes until all the strips are browned, stirring once. Transfer the meat to a plate with a slotted spoon. Repeat with the remaining oil and meat.
2 Tip the mushrooms into the pan, lower the heat a little and fry, stirring occasionally, until they begin to colour (about 5 minutes). Sprinkle in the paprika and stir fry briefly, then tip in the potatoes, passata and enough stock to cover the potatoes. Stir well, cover and simmer for 20 minutes or until the potatoes are tender.
3 Return the meat to the pan with its juices, stir well and simmer for 5 minutes or until tender. Taste for seasoning and serve topped with the yogurt and parsley.

PER SERVING 279 kcals, protein 26g, carbs 25g, fat 9g, sat fat 2.2g, fibre 2g, added sugar 0.9g, salt 0.87g

Guinea fowl with roast chestnuts

Guinea fowl is widely available, but you could easily use a medium-sized chicken in this autumnal one-pot instead.

TAKES 2 HOURS • SERVES 4

1 guinea fowl (or chicken) about 1.3kg/3lb
½ large lemon
2 bay leaves
several fresh thyme sprigs
3 tbsp olive oil
500g/1lb 2oz potatoes, unpeeled, cut into chunks
3 garlic cloves, unpeeled and bruised
200g/7oz chestnut mushrooms, halved if large
200g/7oz vacuum-packed cooked chestnuts
FOR THE SAUCE
150ml/¼ pint white wine
150ml/¼ pint chicken stock
1 tbsp bramble or redcurrant jelly

1 Heat the oven to 190C/170C fan/gas 5. Season the meat, put the lemon half, the bay leaves and two sprigs of thyme inside the bird. Set in a roasting tin, drizzle with a little olive oil, then roast for 15 minutes.
2 Meanwhile, strip the remaining thyme leaves from their stalks. Mix together the potatoes, thyme, garlic and remaining oil, then season. Put the potatoes around the bird, then roast for 45 minutes more.
3 Stir the mushrooms into the potatoes along with the chestnuts. Roast for a further 15 minutes until the mushrooms are cooked. Lift the bird and veg out of the pan on to a serving platter and keep warm.
4 Boil the pan juices on the hob, add the wine, stock and jelly, then bring to the boil, stirring to dissolve the jelly. Boil hard until the sauce is slightly thickened. Season to taste, then serve.

PER SERVING 633 kcals, protein 56g, carbs 45g, fat 24g, sat fat 6g, fibre 5g, sugar 9g, salt 0.56g

Guinea fowl with roast chestnuts

Steak and mushroom goulash

Moroccan lamb harira

This soup is a meal in itself and it's sure to be a hit with its delicious aromas and wonderful flavours.

TAKES 2½–2¾ HOURS • SERVES 8

100g/3½oz dried chickpeas, soaked overnight
    and drained
100g/3½oz Puy lentils
750g/1lb 10oz ready-diced lamb, cut into
    1cm/½in cubes
1 large Spanish onion, finely chopped
1 tsp ground turmeric
½ tsp ground cinnamon
¼ tsp each ground ginger, saffron strands
    and paprika
50g/2oz butter
100g/3½oz long grain rice
4 large ripe tomatoes, peeled, deseeded
    and chopped
2 tbsp chopped fresh coriander
4 tbsp chopped fresh flat-leaf parsley
lemon quarters, to serve

1 Tip the chickpeas and lentils into a large saucepan or flameproof casserole. Add the lamb, onion and spices and pour in about 1.5 litres/2½ pints water – enough to cover the meat and pulses. Season.
2 Bring to the boil, skimming the froth from the surface as the water begins to bubble, then stir in half the butter. Turn down the heat and simmer, covered, for 2 hours until the chickpeas are tender, adding the rice and tomatoes for the last 30 minutes, with more water if necessary.
3 To finish, stir in the remaining butter with the coriander and parsley (hold a little back for a garnish if you like) and taste for seasoning. Serve hot, with a lemon quarter for each serving so guests can squeeze over lemon juice to taste.

PER SERVING 370 kcals, protein 25g, carbs 28g, fat 18g, sat fat 9.2g, fibre 3.6g, added sugar none, salt 0.27g

Fragrant chicken curry

Impress your friends with this sensational curry, which delivers a full, rich flavour and authentic spiciness without the usual high-fat content.

TAKES 1–1¼ HOURS • SERVES 8

3 onions, quartered
4 fat garlic cloves
5cm/2in fresh root ginger, peeled and roughly
    chopped
3 tbsp moglai (medium) curry powder
1 tsp turmeric
2 tsp paprika
2 fresh red chillies, deseeded and roughly
    chopped
2 x 20g packs fresh coriander
1 chicken stock cube
6 large boneless, skinless chicken breasts,
    cubed
2 x 410g cans chickpeas, drained and rinsed
natural low-fat yogurt, naan bread or
    poppadums, to serve

1 Tip the onions, garlic, ginger, curry powder, ground spices, chillies and half the coriander into a food processor. Add 1 teaspoon salt and blend to a purée (you may need to do this in two batches). Tip the mixture into a large saucepan and cook over a low heat for 10 minutes, stirring frequently.
2 Crumble in the stock cube, pour in 750ml/1¼ pints boiling water and return to the boil. Add the chicken, stir, then lower the heat and simmer for 20 minutes or until the chicken is tender.
3 Chop the remaining coriander, then stir all but about 2 tablespoons into the curry with the chickpeas. Heat through. Serve topped with the reserved coriander and the natural yogurt, with naan bread or poppadums on the side.

PER SERVING 227 kcals, protein 32g, carbs 17g, fat 4g, sat fat 0.4g, fibre 4.6g, added sugar none, salt 1.72g

Moroccan lamb harira

Fragrant chicken curry

Chinese-style braised beef

If you know you want to serve a stew but fancy trying something different, this dish is for you. Just serve it with a big bowl of rice.

TAKES ABOUT 2½ HOURS • SERVES 6

3 pak choi heads, halved
3–4 tbsp olive oil
6 garlic cloves, thinly sliced
a good thumb-sized knob of ginger, peeled and shredded
1 bunch spring onions, sliced
1 red chilli, deseeded and thinly sliced
1.5kg/3lb 5oz braising beef, well marbled and cut into large pieces
2 tbsp plain flour, well seasoned
1 tsp Chinese five spice powder
2 star anise
2 tsp light muscovado sugar (or use whatever you've got)
3 tbsp Chinese cooking wine or dry sherry
3 tbsp dark soy sauce, plus more to taste
500ml/18fl oz beef stock

1 Bring 2cm water to boil in a large casserole, then simmer the pak choi for 4 minutes. Drain, cool under cold water; set aside.
2 Heat 2 tablespoons oil in the pan. Fry the garlic, ginger, onions and chilli for 3 minutes then set aside. Toss the beef with flour, add more oil to the pan, then brown in batches, about 5 minutes each time, and set aside.
3 Add the spices, fry for 1 minute, then tip in the gingery mix. Tip in the sugar and beef, then stir. Splash in the wine or sherry. Heat the oven to 150C/130C fan/gas 2.
4 Pour in the soy sauce and stock and boil. Tightly cover the pan then braise in the oven for 1½–2 hours, stirring halfway, until meltingly soft. Nestle the pak choi into the sauce, then leave for a few minutes, lid on, to warm through. Season with extra soy sauce before serving.

PER SERVING 513 kcals, protein 54g, carbs 9g, fat 29g, sat fat 10g, fibre 1g, sugar 4g, salt 2.39g

Thai green chicken curry

Thai curries cook in just a few minutes once all the ingredients are prepared, so this is a one-pot dish you'll be cooking again and again.

TAKES 30–40 MINUTES • SERVES 8

2 tbsp vegetable oil
2 garlic cloves, chopped
6 tsp Thai green curry paste
2 x 400ml cans coconut milk
450g/1lb new potatoes, scrubbed and cut into chunks
200g pack trimmed green beans, halved
4 tsp Thai fish sauce (nam pla), or to taste
2 tsp caster sugar
6 boneless, skinless chicken breasts, cut into large bite-size pieces
2 fresh kaffir lime leaves, finely shredded, or 3 wide strips lime zest
large handful of basil leaves

1 Heat the oil in a large wok, drop in the garlic and stir until just golden. Add the curry paste and stir for a couple of minutes, then pour in the coconut milk and bring to the boil. Add the potatoes and simmer for 10 minutes, then add the beans and simmer for 5 minutes more. Both the potatoes and beans should be just tender by now – if not, cook a little longer.
2 Stir in the fish sauce and sugar, then add the chicken, cover and simmer for 10 minutes until tender. Before serving, stir in the lime leaves or zest, followed by the basil. Taste and add more fish sauce, if you like.

PER SERVING 363 kcals, protein 29g, carbs 15g, fat 21g, sat fat 14.6g, fibre 1.3g, added sugar 1.4g, salt 1.09g

Thai green chicken curry

Chinese-style braised beef

Red wine braised lamb shanks

You'll often see lamb shanks on restaurant menus; this is because they're great value and will transform into a fantastic meal with little effort. Make them the day before for a really full flavour.

TAKES 2½ HOURS • SERVES 4

2 tbsp olive oil
4 lamb shanks
2 large onions, sliced
1 carrot, peeled and sliced
1 celery stick, sliced
2 garlic cloves, sliced
250ml/9fl oz full-bodied red wine
250ml/9fl oz beef or lamb stock
175ml/6fl oz tomato passata
1 tsp golden caster sugar
1 bay leaf
1 fresh thyme sprig
chopped flat-leaf parsley, to garnish

1 Heat the oven to 160C/140C fan/gas 3. Put a large casserole dish over a high heat with 1 tablespoon olive oil. Add the lamb shanks and brown really well on all sides. Remove and set aside.
2 Reduce the heat, add the remaining olive oil and the sliced onions, carrot and celery. Cook for 5 minutes until the vegetables are mostly tender. Add the garlic and continue to cook for a further minute.
3 Pour the red wine into the pan, boil, then simmer for 3 minutes. Add the stock, passata, sugar, bay leaf, thyme and seasoning, and bring back to the boil. Add the lamb shanks, coating them in the braising liquid. Cover with a tight-fitting lid and braise for about 2 hours or until the meat is really tender, turning the meat in the liquid every 30 minutes. Check the seasoning, scatter with parsley and serve.

PER SERVING 460 kcals, protein 37g, carbs 15g, fat 24g, sat fat 10g, fibre 3g, added sugar 2g, salt 1g

Pork with celeriac and orange

This is the magic formula for making cheaper cuts of meat meltingly tender.

TAKES 2½–2¾ HOURS • SERVES 8

1kg/2lb 4oz boneless pork shoulder, cut into bite-size chunks
3 tbsp olive oil
1 large celeriac (about 1kg/2lb 4oz) peeled and chopped into large chunks
4 leeks, trimmed and chopped into chunks
3 carrots, peeled and chopped into chunks
2 garlic cloves, chopped
400ml/14fl oz dry white wine
400ml/14fl oz chicken stock
2 tbsp soy sauce
finely grated zest and juice 1 large orange
large rosemary sprig

1 Heat the oven to 140C/120C fan/gas 1. Season the meat well then heat 1 tablespoon of the oil in a large flameproof casserole over a medium-high heat. Add half the pork and leave for a couple of minutes until browned underneath, then brown the other side for 2–3 minutes. Using a slotted spoon, transfer the pork to a plate. Repeat with another spoonful of oil and the remaining meat.
2 Heat the remaining oil in the pan and fry the vegetables and garlic for 3–4 minutes until starting to brown. Tip the pork and its juices into the pan, then add the remaining ingredients. Stir well and bring to the boil.
3 Cover the pan and cook in the oven for 2–2¼ hours until the pork is very tender, stirring halfway. Leave to stand for 10 minutes, taste for seasoning and serve.

PER SERVING 251 kcals, protein 29g, carbs 11g, fat 10g, sat fat 2.3g, fibre 6.9g, added sugar 0.1g, salt 1.39g

Pork with celeriac and orange

Red wine braised lamb shanks

Chicken with goat's cheese

This dish tastes rather special for something that's so easy to make. As an alternative to goat's cheese you can use garlic soft cheese.

TAKES 40–50 MINUTES • SERVES 8

8 large skinless chicken breasts
20g pack fresh tarragon
2 x 150g cartons soft goat's cheese
5 vine-ripened tomatoes, sliced
3 tbsp olive oil
dressed salad leaves and bread, to serve

1 Heat the oven to 200C/180C fan/gas 6. Make a slit down the centre of each chicken breast (taking care not to cut right through), then make a pocket with your fingers. Arrange the chicken in a single layer in a large, lightly oiled ovenproof dish.
2 Reserve eight sprigs of tarragon, chop the rest of the leaves and beat into the cheese with plenty of black pepper. Spoon into the pockets in the chicken. Place 2 tomato slices over each cheese-filled pocket, put a tarragon sprig on top and drizzle with oil.
3 Season and bake for 25–30 minutes until the chicken is cooked, but still moist. Serve hot or cold with dressed salad leaves and bread.

PER SERVING 248 kcals, protein 34g, carbs 2g, fat 12g, sat fat 4g, fibre 1g, added sugar none, salt 0.64g

Beef paprikash

A comforting and hearty dish that's perfect for winter dinner parties.

TAKES 3–3½ HOURS • SERVES 8

3 tbsp sunflower oil
1.5kg/3lb braising steak or stewing beef, cut into 5cm/2in cubes
2 large onions, sliced
2 garlic cloves, crushed
2 rounded tbsp paprika
3 tbsp tomato purée
2 tbsp wine vinegar (red or white)
2 tsp dried marjoram or mixed herbs
2 bay leaves
½ tsp caraway seeds
2 x 400g cans chopped tomatoes or 2 x 500g jars passata
750ml/1¼ pints beef stock
2 large red peppers, deseeded and cut into rings
142ml pot soured cream

1 Heat the oven to 160C/140C fan/gas 3. Heat 2 tablespoons of the oil in a large flameproof casserole until very hot. Brown the meat in 2–3 batches, removing each batch with a slotted spoon.
2 Add the remaining oil, the onions and garlic. Cook on a low heat for 10 minutes, stirring now and then, until the onions soften. Add the meat and juices, and blend in the paprika, tomato purée, vinegar, herbs, bay leaves and caraway seeds.
3 Tip in the tomatoes, add the stock, season and bring to the boil, adding some water if the meat is not covered. Stir, cover, and put in the oven for 2½ hours, or until the meat is tender. Halfway through, stir in the red peppers. Serve with dollops of soured cream.

PER SERVING 451 kcals, protein 43g, carbs 14g, fat 25g, sat fat 9.7g, fibre 2.8g, added sugar none, salt 0.87g

Beef and bean hotpot

This is a brilliant way of stretching a couple of packets of mince.

TAKES ABOUT 1 HOUR • SERVES 8

750g/1lb 10oz lean minced beef
1 beef stock cube
2 large onions, roughly chopped
450g/1lb carrots, peeled and thickly sliced
1.25kg/2lb 8oz potatoes, peeled and cut
    into large chunks
2 x 400g cans baked beans
Worcestershire sauce or Tabasco, to taste
large handful of parsley, roughly chopped

1 Heat a large non-stick pan, add the beef and fry over a medium-high heat until browned, stirring often and breaking up any lumps with a spoon. Crumble in the stock cube and mix well.
2 Add the vegetables, stir to mix with the beef and pour in enough boiling water (about 1.2 litres/2 pints) to cover. Bring to the boil, then lower the heat and stir well. Cover the pan and simmer gently for about 30 minutes or until the vegetables are tender.
3 Tip in the baked beans, sprinkle with Worcestershire or Tabasco sauce to taste, stir well and heat through. Taste for seasoning and sprinkle with the parsley. Serve with extra Worcestershire or Tabasco sauce, for those who like a peppery hot taste.

PER SERVING 362 kcals, protein 31g, carbs 51g, fat 5g, sat fat 1.9g, fibre 7.9g, added sugar 3.4g, salt 2.05g

Chilli con carne

A great chilli has to be one of the best dishes to serve to friends for a casual get-together, and this one is even better made in advance.

TAKES ABOUT 1¼ HOURS • SERVES 8

2 tbsp vegetable oil
1 large Spanish onion, finely chopped
2 red peppers, deseeded and cut into 1cm/½in
    dice
2 garlic cloves, crushed
1–2 tsp chilli powder, to taste
2 tsp paprika
2 tsp ground cumin
1 tsp dried marjoram
900g/2lb minced beef
1 beef stock cube
2 x 400g cans chopped tomatoes
3 tbsp tomato purée
1 tsp sugar
2 x 410g cans red kidney beans, drained and
    rinsed

1 Heat the oil in a large, deep pan and gently fry the onion until softened. Add the red peppers, garlic, spices and marjoram and fry, stirring, for 5 minutes. Tip in the meat and increase the heat to high. Fry until all of the meat is browned, stirring often and breaking up any lumps with a spoon.
2 Crumble in the stock cube and pour in 600ml/ 1 pint water, then tip in the tomatoes and add the tomato purée and sugar. Stir well and bring to the boil. Cover and simmer for 30 minutes, stirring in a splash or two of hot water from the kettle if the meat becomes dry.
3 Stir in the beans and heat through, uncovered, for 10 minutes. Remove from the heat and taste for seasoning, then cover the pan. Leave to stand for 10–15 minutes before serving.

PER SERVING 402 kcals, protein 30g, carbs 22g, fat 22g, sat fat 8.5g, fibre 6.3g, added sugar 0.7g, salt 1.61g

Sticky cinnamon figs, page 182

Desserts

Beaujolais berries

Marinating the strawberries in the Beaujolais gives them a lovely flavour, but don't do it too far ahead or they will lose their texture.

TAKES 5–10 MINUTES, PLUS MARINATING • SERVES 6

700g/1lb 9oz strawberries, hulled and halved
3 tbsp golden caster sugar
handful of mint leaves, plus a few extra
½ 75cl bottle Beaujolais

1 Lay the strawberries in a bowl and sprinkle over the caster sugar. Scatter over handful of mint leaves and let the strawberries sit for about 30 minutes so they start to release their juices.
2 Pour the Beaujolais over the strawberries and scatter over a few more fresh mint leaves. Leave for another 10 minutes before serving.

PER SERVING 102 kcals, protein 1g, carbs 15g, fat 1g, sat fat none, fibre 1g, added sugar 8g, salt 0.03g

Tropical fruit salad

The lovely colours and fabulous flavours of this one-pot pudding will really surprise you.

TAKES 25–30 MINUTES • SERVES 4

1 ripe papaya
1 small pineapple
12 Cape gooseberries (physalis)
50g/2oz butter
4 tbsp light or dark muscovado sugar
4 tbsp coconut rum (or white or dark rum) or
    pineapple and coconut juice
seeds of 1 pomegranate
vanilla or rum and raisin ice cream, to serve

1 Halve the papaya lengthways and scoop out the seeds, then peel the fruit and cut into slim wedges. Cut off the top, bottom and skin of the pineapple, and remove all the eyes from the flesh. Cut the pineapple lengthways into wedges and slice the core off the edge of each wedge. Cut each wedge crossways into chunks. Remove the papery husks from the cape gooseberries.
2 Melt the butter and sugar in a wide, deep pan, add the prepared fruit and toss until coated and glistening. Sprinkle over the rum or fruit juice and the pomegranate seeds, and shake the pan to distribute evenly. Serve hot, with ice cream.

PER SERVING 308 kcals, protein 2g, carbs 45g, fat 11g, sat fat 6.5g, fibre 4.8g, added sugar 15.2g, salt 0.22g

Beaujolais berries

Tropical fruit salad

Cherry vanilla clafoutis

Serve the clafoutis barely warm to get the best from the subtle flavours.

TAKES 1–1¼ HOURS • SERVES 6

650g/1lb 7oz fresh cherries (dark, juicy ones)
4 tbsp golden caster sugar
4 tbsp kirsch
3 eggs
50g/2oz plain flour
150ml/¼ pint milk
200ml carton crème fraîche (full or half fat)
1 tsp vanilla extract
icing sugar, for dusting

1 Heat the oven to 190C/170C fan/gas 5. Stone the cherries, but try to keep them whole.
2 Scatter the cherries over the base of a buttered shallow ovenproof dish, about 1 litre capacity. Sprinkle the cherries with 1 tablespoon each of sugar and kirsch.
3 Whisk the eggs with an electric beater or hand whisk until they are soft and foamy – about 1–2 minutes. Whisk in the flour and remaining sugar, then add the remaining kirsch, the milk, crème fraîche and vanilla extract.
4 Pour the batter over the cherries and bake for 35–40 minutes until pale golden. Leave to cool to room temperature, then dust lightly with icing sugar and serve just warm.

PER SERVING 309 kcals, protein 7g, carbs 35g, fat 14g, sat fat 7g, fibre 1g, added sugar 15g, salt 0.23g

Simple summer pudding

To make small puddings, simply tear the bread roughly and layer up with the fruit in individual ramekins. Turn out or serve as they are.

TAKES 40–50 MINUTES • SERVES 4

450g/1lb summer berries, defrosted if frozen
4 tbsp blackcurrant cordial or crème de cassis
225g carton chilled red fruits compote
6 medium slices white bread, crusts cut off

1 Mix the berries, cordial and compote or creme de cassis and leave for 5–10 minutes. If you are using defrosted fruit, mix in some of the juice.
2 Line a 1.2 litre pudding bowl with cling film, letting it hang over the sides. Cut a circle from one of the slices of bread to fit the base of the bowl, then cut the remaining slices into quarters.
3 Drain the juice from the fruit into a bowl and dip the bread into it until soaked. Layer the fruit and bread in the bowl and pour over the remaining juice. Cover with the overhanging cling film. Put a small plate or saucer on top to fit inside the rim of the bowl, then stand a couple of heavy cans on top to press it down. Chill in the refrigerator for at least 10 minutes, or until you are ready to eat (it will keep for up to 24 hours).

PER SERVING 201 kcals, protein 5g, carbs 46g, fat 1g, sat fat 0.2g, fibre 5g, added sugar 11g, salt 0.6g

Simple summer pudding

Cherry vanilla clafoutis

Dark chocolate fondue with crushed nuts and tropical fruits

Any selection of fruit works with this dip. Try berries in the summer or marshmallows and bite-size pieces of cake in colder months.

TAKES 15 MINUTES • SERVES 4

200g/7oz plain chocolate
50g/2oz butter
2 tbsp Malibu or white rum
½ mango, peeled and cubed
½ papaya, peeled and cubed
8 physalis (also known as Cape gooseberries)
200g pack pineapple chunks (or cut your own fresh pineapple)
50g/2oz toasted crushed hazelnuts

1 Put the chocolate, butter, alcohol and 75ml/ 2½fl oz water into a heatproof bowl set above a pan of gently simmering water. Make sure the bottom of the bowl doesn't touch the water. Let it sit for 5–10 minutes, stirring occasionally until smooth.
2 Arrange the fruit on a platter with a bowl of the crushed nuts and forks or cocktail sticks ready for dipping. Dip the fruit chunks into the chocolate and then the nuts, and pop them straight into your mouth (or someone else's!).

PER SERVING 505 kcals, protein 5g, carbs 47g, fat 32g, sat fat 15g, fibre 4g, sugar 46g, salt 0.21g

Broken biscotti ice cream with hot mocha

Give ice cream an Italian twist with this easy coffee-flavoured chocolatey dessert. It's so good you might want to make double!

TAKES 10 MINUTES • SERVES 4

500ml tub good-quality vanilla ice cream
12 biscotti biscuits
100g bar good-quality dark chocolate
2 tbsp brandy
200ml/7fl oz (about 1 mug) freshly made strong coffee

1 Leave the ice cream out of the freezer for 5 minutes to soften, then tip into a bowl. Put six of the biscuits into a freezer bag, squeeze out the air, then bash the biscuits into crumbs. Fold into the ice cream then return to the freezer.
2 Break the chocolate into a pan, add the brandy and heat gently until melted. Stir (it will thicken), then pour in the hot coffee and carry on stirring until it becomes a smooth mocha.
3 Scoop the ice cream into heatproof glasses or bowls, then pour the mocha over. Serve straight away with the remaining biscotti on the side.

PER SERVING 349 kcals, protein 6g, carbs 38g, fat 19g, sat fat 11g, fibre 2g, sugar 26g, salt 0.26g

Dark chocolate fondue with crushed nuts
and tropical fruits

Broken biscotti ice cream with hot mocha

Grilled summer berry pudding

This recipe has all the elements of a summer pudding, but is much simpler, and served hot. The jammy smells as it cooks are wonderful.

TAKES 20–30 MINUTES • SERVES 4

4 slices white sliced bread, crusts removed
85g/3oz golden caster sugar
2 tsp cornflour
200g carton low-fat fromage frais
300g/10oz mixed summer berries (such as
    raspberries, blueberries, redcurrants,
    sliced strawberries) or 300g/10oz frozen
    berries, defrosted

1 Heat the grill to high. Lay the slices of bread slightly overlapping in a shallow flameproof dish. Sprinkle about 2 tablespoons of the sugar over the bread and grill for about 2 minutes until the bread is toasted and the sugar is starting to caramelise. Mix the cornflour into the fromage frais.
2 Pile the fruit down the middle of the bread and sprinkle with 1 tablespoon of the sugar. Drop spoonfuls of the fromage frais mixture on top, then sprinkle over the rest of the sugar.
3 Put the dish as close to the heat as you can and grill for 6–8 minutes until the fromage frais has browned and everything else is starting to bubble and turn juicy. Leave for a minute or two before serving.

PER SERVING 211 kcals, protein 7g, carbs 47g, fat 1g, sat fat none, fibre 2g, added sugar 22g, salt 0.45g

Sticky cinnamon figs

Splash a few tablespoons of Armagnac or brandy over the figs before grilling to make a boozy pudding.

TAKES 10 MINUTES • SERVES 4

8 ripe figs
large knob of butter
4 tbsp clear honey
handful shelled pistachio nuts or almonds
1 tsp ground cinnamon or mixed spice
mascarpone or Greek yogurt, to serve

1 Heat the grill to medium high. Cut a deep cross in the top of each fig, then ease the top apart like a flower. Sit the figs in a baking dish and drop a small piece of the butter into the centre of each fruit. Drizzle the honey over the figs, then sprinkle with the nuts and spice.
2 Grill for 5 minutes until the figs are softened and the honey and butter make a sticky sauce in the bottom of the dish. Serve warm, with dollops of mascarpone or yogurt.

PER SERVING 162 kcals, protein 3g, carbs 23g, fat 7g, sat fat 2g, fibre 2g, added sugar 11.5g, salt 0.06g

Grilled summer berry pudding

Sticky cinnamon figs

Rhubarb, ginger and apple scrunch pie

This is the ultimate cheat's dessert; it tastes every bit as gorgeous as a full-blown fruit pie, without all the work and washing up.

TAKES 1 HOUR • SERVES 6

butter, for greasing
375g pack ready-rolled shortcrust pastry
400g/14oz Bramley apples, sliced
400g pack trimmed rhubarb, cut into lengths
100g/3½oz demerara sugar, plus extra for
    sprinkling
2 balls stem ginger, chopped
2 tbsp cornflour
milk, for brushing
custard, to serve

1 Heat the oven to 180C/160C fan/gas 4 and grease a large baking sheet. Unroll the pastry and place it flat on the baking sheet.
2 Mix the apple slices and the rhubarb with the sugar, ginger and cornflour, then pile into the centre of the pastry. Gather up the sides of the pastry to enclose the fruit so that the pie looks like a rough tart (you need to work with the size and shape of the pastry, so it will be more of an oblong shape than round).
3 Brush the pastry with milk and scatter with demerara. Bake for 35 minutes until the pastry is golden and the fruit is tender. Cut into slices and serve with custard.

PER SERVING 397 kcals, protein 4g, carbs 59g, fat 18g, sat fat 9g, fibre 4g, added sugar 18g, salt 0.27g

Star anise and lemon pears

Gently infused spice transforms the humble pear into a wonderful winter dessert. Serve with scoops of ice cream or a drizzle of cream.

TAKES 1 HOUR • SERVES 4

zest and juice 1 lemon
140g/5oz golden caster sugar
4 star anise
4 ripe pears

1 Thinly peel the zest from the lemon with a potato peeler and put the zest in a pan with the sugar, star anise and 1 litre/1¾ pints water. Bring to the boil, then leave to infuse for 5 minutes.
2 Peel and core the pears, leaving the stem on, then lower into the syrup. Cover and leave to cook on a gentle heat for 10 minutes or until the pears are tender. Lift the pears from the pan, then boil the liquid over a high heat until syrupy. Squeeze the juice from the lemon into the syrup, then pour over the pears. Eat warm or chilled.

PER SERVING 205 kcals, protein 1g, carbs 53g, fat none, sat fat none, fibre 3g, added sugar 37g, salt 0.02g

Rhubarb, ginger and apple scrunch pie

Star anise and lemon pears

Cookie-dough crumble

To make this tasty pudding extra fruity, slice up a couple of pears or a cooking apple (with a sprinkling of sugar) and stir into the fruit.

TAKES 20–25 MINUTES • SERVES 4

500g bag mixed frozen fruit
350g pot fresh cookie dough (chocolate chip is good)
cream, ice cream or custard, to serve

1 Heat the oven to 220C/200C fan/gas 7. Tip the frozen fruit into a shallow baking dish and tear pieces of dough all over the top.
2 Bake for 20 minutes until crisp and golden. Serve with cream, ice cream or custard.

PER SERVING 457 kcals, protein 8g, carbs 57g, fat 24g, sat fat 13g, fibre 6g, added sugar 9g, salt 1.2g

Plum and marzipan tarte Tatin

Choose firm plums for this recipe – if they are overripe they will ooze too much juice and you will have a flood on your kitchen worktop.

TAKES ABOUT 1–1¼ HOURS • SERVES 6–8

25g/1oz butter
25g/1oz golden caster sugar
800g/1lb 12oz firm plums, not too ripe, halved and stoned
100g/3½oz golden marzipan
40g/1½oz ground almonds
500g pack puff pastry, thawed if frozen
pouring cream (single or double), to serve

1 Heat the oven to 200C/180C fan/gas 6. Melt the butter in a 28cm/11in tarte Tatin tin over a medium heat. Tip in the sugar and 1 tablespoon water and stir for a few minutes until lightly browned. Remove from the heat and put in the plums, cut side up.
2 Chop the marzipan into as many chunks as there are plum halves, put a chunk into each plum and sprinkle over the ground almonds.
3 Roll out the pastry and trim to 4cm/1½in larger than the tin all round. Lift the pastry onto the tin and tuck it down between the plums and the inside of the tin. Bake for 30–35 minutes until the pastry is risen, crisp and golden. Cool for 10 minutes, then place a large flat plate with a rim over the tin. Holding it over the sink in case of drips, invert the tarte on to the plate. Serve with cream.

PER SERVING for six 511 kcals, protein 8g, carbs 58g, fat 29g, sat fat 3g, fibre 3g, added sugar 13g, salt 0.75g

Plum and marzipan tarte Tatin

Cookie-dough crumble

Tiramisu trifle

Everyone will fall in love with this recipe! It's hard to believe that something that tastes this good can take so little time and effort to make.

TAKES 10–15 MINUTES, PLUS CHILLING • SERVES 8–10

300ml/½ pint strong, good-quality black coffee
175ml/6fl oz amaretto liqueur
500g carton mascarpone
500g/1lb 2oz good-quality fresh custard
250g/9oz Savoiardi biscuits (Italian sponge
    fingers) or sponge fingers
85g/3oz good-quality dark chocolate, roughly
    chopped
TO DECORATE
4 tbsp toasted slivered almonds
chopped dark chocolate

1 Mix the coffee and liqueur in a wide dish. Beat the mascarpone and custard together in a bowl with a hand blender or whisk.
2 Take a third of the sponge fingers and dip each one into the coffee mix until soft but not soggy. Line the bottom of a glass trifle dish with the biscuits and drizzle over more of the coffee mixture.
3 Sprinkle a third of the chocolate over the biscuits, then follow with a layer of the mascarpone mixture. Repeat twice more. Chill in the fridge for at least 2 hours (preferably overnight). Sprinkle with the almonds and chocolate before serving.

PER SERVING for eight 624 kcals, protein 8g, carbs 54g, fat 39g, sat fat 23g, fibre 1g, added sugar 35g, salt 0.38g

Spicy steamed fruit pudding

This special treat of a dessert makes a good alternative to Christmas pudding. Serve it with crème fraîche or vanilla ice cream.

TAKES 2½–3 HOURS • SERVES 8–10

1 cup raisins
1 cup sultanas
1 cup self-raising flour
1 cup finely grated cold butter (about
    100g/3½oz), plus extra at room temperature
    for greasing
1 cup fresh brown breadcrumbs (from around
    4 thick slices bread)
1 cup light muscovado sugar
1 cup mixed nuts, chopped (optional)
1 tsp ground cinnamon
1 tsp ground mixed spice
1 cup milk
1 egg
TO SERVE (OPTIONAL)
butterscotch or caramel sauce
handful of mixed nuts

1 Using a 300ml/½ pint coffee mug as your cup measure, empty the first 6 cups and the nuts, if using, into a bowl with the spices, then stir in the milk and egg until well combined. Tip into a buttered 1.5 litre/2¾ pint pudding bowl.
2 Cover with a double layer of buttered foil, making a pleat in the centre to allow the pudding to rise. Tie with string, then place in a steamer or large pan with enough gently simmering water to come halfway up the sides of the bowl. Cover and steam for 2½ hours, adding more water as necessary.
3 To serve, unwrap the pudding and invert on to a deep plate, then drizzle with sauce and decorate the top with nuts, if using.

PER SERVING for eight 423 kcals, protein 6g, carbs 75g, fat 13g, sat fat 7.9g, fibre 1.8g, added sugar 28.5g, salt 0.66g

Tiramisu trifle

Spicy steamed fruit pudding

Index

Picture credits

BBC *Good Food* magazine and BBC Books would like to thank the following people for providing photos. While every effort has been made to trace and acknowledge all photographers, we should like to apologise should their be any errors or omissions.

page 8 Myles New & Craig Robertson; 11t Jason Lowe; 11b William Longwood; 13t Iain Bagwell; 13b Philip Webb; 15t David Munns; 15b David Munns; 19t Ken Field; 19b Steve Baxter; 21t Myles New; 21b Lis Parsons; 23t Ken Field; 23b Roger Stowell; 27t Lis Parsons; 27b Myles New; 29t Lis Parsons; 29b Peter Cassidy; 31t Lis Parsons; 31b David Munns; 33t David Munns; 33b Gareth Morgans; 35t Myles New; 35b Roger Stowell; 38 Myles New; 41t Lis Parsons; 41b Yuki Sigiura; 43t Lis Parsons; 43b David Munns; 45t Ken Field; 45b xxx; 49t Roger Stowell; 49b David Munns; 51t Myles New; 51b Myles New; 53t Philip Webb; 53b Philip Webb; 57t Myles New; 57b Lis Parsons; 59t Roger Stowell; 59b Philip Webb; 61t Peter Cassidy; 61b Philip Webb; 65t; Yuki Sugiura; 65b Marie-Louise Avery; 67t Roger Stowell; 67b Steve Baxter; 69t Lis Parsons; 69b David Munns; 73t Jonathan Whittaker; 73b Roger Stowell; 75t Debi Treloar; 75b Kate Whitaker; 77t Simon Walton; 77b Dawie Verwey; 81t; Philip Webb 81b Myles New; 83t Peter Cassidy; 83b David Munns; 86 Philip Webb; 89t Philip Webb; 89b Howard Shooter; 91t Philip Webb; 91b Gareth Morgans; 93t Roger Stowell; 93b Roger Stowell; 95t Steve Baxter; 95b Roger Stowell; 99t Ken

Field; 99b Iain Bagwell; 101t David Munns; 101b Simon Wheeler; 103t Myles New; 103b William Lingwood; 105t Kate Whitaker; 105b Peter Cassidy; 107t Lis Parsons; 107b Lis Parsons; 109t Gareth Morgans; 109b Ken Field; 111t Lis Parsons; 111b David Munns; 113t Philip Webb; 113b Myles New; 115t Roger Stowell; 115b Ken Field; 118 Ken Field; 121t Marie-Louise Avery; 121b Gareth Morgans; 123t Peter Cassidy; 123b Myles New; 127t David Munns; 127b Cameron Watt; 129t Myles New; 129b Lis Parsons; 131b Philip Webb; 133t Myles New; 133b Sharon Smith; 135t Roger Stowell; 135b Roger Stowell; 137t David King; 137b Ken Field; 139t Roger Stowell; 139b David Munns; 141t Lis Parsons; 141b Myles New; 143t Marie-Louise Avery; 143b Lis Parsons; 145t Simon Wheeler; 145b Roger Stowell; 147t Myles New; 147b David Munns; 150 Myles New; 153t Philip Webb; 153b Philip Webb; 155t Debi Treloar; 155b David Munns; 157t Brett Stevens; 157b Philip Webb; 159t Myles New; 159b Lis Parsons; 161t David Munns; 161b Ken Field; 165t Roger Stowell; 165b Philip Webb; 167t Martin Brigdale; 167b Simon Wheeler; 169t Simon Walton; 169b Peter Cassidy; 171t Carl Clemens-Gros; 171b Cameron Watt; 174 Will Heap; 177t Simon Wheeler; 177b Craig Robertson; 179t Jason Lowe; 179b Roger Stowell; 181t Myles New; 181b David Munns; 183t David Munns; 183b Will Heap; 185t Peter Cassidy; 185b Peter Cassidy; 187t Simon Wheeler; 187b Philip Webb; 189t Craig Robertson; 189b Roger Stowell.